Dr Ravindra Sharma, a native of Jammu, India, is a surgeon by profession, having retired as professor of surgery. He picked up the basic elements of astrology from his father, Pt Rup Chand Ji Sharma, a renowned Ayurvedic physician of Jammu, at the age of 12. He became ill at the age of 17 when he was a 1st-year medical student at Amritsar. The illness resulted in a prolonged stay at Jammu. This led him to consult his uncle for advice. His uncle, Pt Madan Mohan Ji Shastri, a Jyotishacharya, was a Raj Jyotshi and a famous astrologer. In his curiosity to know the reason for his illness, he learnt the basic principles of astrology from his uncle and acquired a life-long interest in the ancient science of astrology.

During the 7 years of stay at Amritsar for medical studies, he came across a number of local astrologers, notable among them being Pt Devi Dass Ji and Professor M. L. Bhatia of DAV College. They were well-known astrologers of Amritsar and his regular interactions with them enhanced his interest and knowledge further in this hobby.

Later, during the pursuit of surgical studies in London, he came in contact with Mr M. K. Gandhi, a well-known Indian astrologer based in London. He developed a close family friendship with Mr Gandhi due to his keen interest and passion for this hobby. Mr Gandhi was an internationally acclaimed astrologer at the time. Many famous public figures of London at the time were his clients. His expert counsel was keenly sought after by the mighty and the rich. His fame led him to undertake several world tours to the USA, Europe, Africa and India, and he had many millionaires among his clients. The author had regular interactions with his friend for an extended period of well over 10 years and added many finer points and subtle nuances of astrology in his repertoire.

As a practising surgeon, he kept alive his interest and passion for his hobby through regular interactions with contemporary hobbyists. Well known among them were Mr K. N. Bhakri and Shri Vidya Vinayak Ji Sharma. Mr Bhakri, a retired Tehsildar, had made quite a name for himself in the higher echelons of administration for his uncanny knowledge and skills. Shri Vinayak Sharma Ji, the younger brother of the author, had learnt astrology from late Master Phool Chand Ji, a famous astrologer of Jammu. He had enhanced his knowledge further by his own studies and research. The author has continued to interact regularly with his brother on astrology for well over 40 years. Their mutual discussions on horoscopes of different people on an almost daily basis would bring out some intricate points of this science and have helped to broaden the base of their hobby. Besides, the author, through his own practice of looking at the horoscopes of his professional colleagues and their families, his own friends and relatives, has maintained his interest in this fulfilling and absorbing hobby.

The author has been a keen and a passionate student of astrology for most of his life. He has pursued this hobby in a quiet and unobtrusive manner for well over 50 years through his personal study, research and practice.

The book is dedicated to my wife, Dr Primla Sharma; our three children, Avneesh, Punam and Atulya; and my late father, Pandit Rup Chand Ji Vaidya.

Dr Ravindra Sharma

A B C OF INDIAN ASTROLOGY

AUSTIN MACAULEY PUBLISHERS™
LONDON · CAMBRIDGE · NEW YORK · SHARJAH

Copyright © Dr Ravindra Sharma (2020)

The right of Dr Ravindra Sharma to be identified as the author of this work has been asserted by the author in accordance with section 77 and 78 of the Copyright, Designs and Patents Act 1988.

All rights reserved. No part of this publication may be reproduced, stored in a retrieval system, or transmitted in any form or by any means, electronic, mechanical, photocopying, recording, or otherwise, without the prior permission of the publishers.

Any person who commits any unauthorised act in relation to this publication may be liable to criminal prosecution and civil claims for damages.

The story, experiences, and words are author's alone.

A CIP catalogue record for this title is available from the British Library.

ISBN 9781528935401 (Paperback)
ISBN 9781528935418 (Hardback)
ISBN 9781528968249 (ePub e-book)

www.austinmacauley.com

First Published (2020)
Austin Macauley Publishers Ltd
25 Canada Square
Canary Wharf
London
E14 5LQ

I would like to thank my uncle, Pandit Madan Mohan Ji Shastri Jyotishacharya; my brother, Shri Vidya Vinayak Ji Sharma; and my astrologer friends, late Mr M. K. Gandhi of London, Prof M. L. Bhatia and Pt Devi Dayal Ji of Amritsar, Pt Raghunath of Srinagar and Mr K.N. Bhakri of Jammu. They not only inspired me in the pursuit of this hobby but also supported and sustained my enthusiasm and passion for this exciting and fascinating science by regular, intensive interactions over many years.

Table of Contents

Preface	**11**
Chapter 1	**13**
Planets and Nodes	
Zodiacal Signs	14
Exaltation of Planets	15
Peak Strength (*Mool-Trikon*) of Planets	15
Debilitation of Planets	16
Friendly Signs of Planets	16
Inimical Signs of Planets	17
Neutral Signs of Planets	18
Effects of Planets Depending on Their Signs	22
Aspects of Planets (Drishti)	26
Special Aspects of Planets:	27
Chapter II	**30**
Horoscope Chart	
12 Houses and Their Portfolios	31
Names of Various Horoscope Charts and Their Relative Importance in Prediction	35
Movement of Planets in a Horoscope Chart	37
Configuration of 30 Degrees in a House of a Horoscope Chart	39
Chapter III	**41**
Zodiacal Signs	
Characteristics of Twelve Zodiacal Signs	42

Effects of Placement of Different Zodiacal Signs in 1st House or Ascendant	43
Chapter IV	**49**
Predictions	
Effects of Placement of Lords of the Twelve Houses of Horoscope	
Chapter V	**68**
Constellations or Nakshtryas	
Names and Characteristics of 27 *Nakshtryas*	71
Chapter VI	**79**
Yogas	
Some of the Important Yogas and Their Effects	79
Chapter VII	**91**
Prediction or Phaladesh[*], Art and Science of Prediction	
Familiarity with Indian Almanac, *Panchang* or *Jantri*	92
Different Horoscope Charts	96
Concept of Benefic and Malefic Planets	97
General Assessment of 12 Houses of a Horoscope Chart	97
Detailed Systematic Assessment of the twelve houses of Horoscope chart	104
Dasha/Antardasha or Reigning Period of Planets in the life of an Individual.	111
Miscellaneous Issues:	120
Answering questions by *Prashna Kundli*	120
Matching Horoscopes of Boy and Girl for Matrimony	121
My today	122
Some Illustrating Horoscopes	128

Preface

This book is written for a lay person in a simple and easy to understand language in order to arouse an interest in the old and ancient science of Indian astrology. Since the beginning of time, man has always wondered whether the heavenly bodies or the planets exercise any influence on the life and destiny of human beings. Through a lot of research, mathematical calculations on the movements of planets, careful analysis of the fluctuating events in the lives and fortunes of human beings and attempting an understanding of their relationship, the ancients of India had divinised that the fortunes and the events in the life of man are indeed significantly shaped by stellar movements. They went on to evolve a system of the art and science of astrology based on their research extended over several centuries. Astrology is not an exact science like Chemistry or Physics. It is as much an art as a science of understanding the influence of planetary movements on the lives of human beings and predicting the course of events in the future. Indeed, the predictions based on this system are remarkably accurate and startlingly revealing.

The Indian system of astrology recognises seven planets and the two nodes of Rahu and Ketu. The sphere of heavenly space around us consists of 360 degrees and has been divided into twelve zodiacal signs of 30 degrees each. In the course of their orbital rotation, the planets transit through these twelve zodiacal signs in an orderly manner. The movement and the placement of planets in different houses and signs is worked out by precise mathematical calculations. The degrees and presence of a planet in a specific house of the horoscope chart exerts a significant influence on the life of a person.

The horoscope chart is prepared on the basis of an individual's time and place of birth. It is based on the placement and degrees of the planet in the heavenly space at the time of birth. The horoscope chart is made up of twelve houses. Each house has well-defined functions and portfolios. An astrological assessment of the horoscope chart enables one to make predictions about the life of an individual.

The author has pursued this fascinating subject as a hobby for well over 50 years and has found it remarkably satisfying and rewarding in answering many of the queries regarding future events. It is with the intention of arousing a similar interest in a common person in the ancient art and science of Indian astrology that he has undertaken the task of bringing out this book.

Chapter 1
Planets and Nodes

There are seven planets and two nodes in the Indian system of astrology. The superior (upper) and the inferior (lower) intersections of the orbits of moon and earth denote the "nodes" and these are known as Rahu and Ketu respectively.

For the purpose of this book, Rahu and Ketu would be considered as planets along with the other seven planets. The words "planet" and "star" are being used synonymously in the book.

The list of the nine planets used in astrology are listed hereunder:

Name of the planet (English)	Name of the planet (Hindi)	Abbreviation
Sun	Surya	Su
Moon	Chandra	Mo
Mars	Mangal	Ma
Mercury	Budh	Me
Jupiter	Brihaspati	Ju
Venus	Shukra	Ve
Saturn	Shanishchra	Sa
Rahu	Rahu	Ra
Ketu	Ketu	K$_E$

Zodiacal Signs

There are twelve zodiacal signs corresponding to the twelve-fold division of space around us. Each of these signs occupies or straddles a space of 30 degrees in the overall space of 360 degrees around us. These twelve signs are assigned the following names and numbers:

Zodiacal Sign (English)	Zodiacal Sign (Hindi)	Sign Number
Aries	*Mesha*	1
Taurus	*Vrikha*	2
Gemini	*Mithun*	3
Cancer	*Karak*	4
Leo	*Singha*	5
Virgo	*Kanya*	6
Libra	*Tula*	7
Scorpio	*Vrishchak*	8
Sagittarius	*Dhan*	9
Capricorn	*Makar*	10
Aquarius	*Kumbh*	11
Pisces	*Meen*	12

These zodiacal signs are referred to simply as signs in the book.

Rulership or Lordship of Different Zodiacal Signs by Planets

1. Sun is the lord of sign Leo (*Sinh*) from 21 to 30 degrees.
2. Moon is the lord of sign Cancer (*Karak*) from 1 to 30 degrees.
3. Mars is the lord of sign Aries (*Mesh*) from 19 to 30 degrees and sign Scorpio (*Vrishchak*) from 1 to 30 degrees.

4. Mercury is the lord of signs Gemini (*Mithun*) from 1 to 30 degrees and Virgo (*Kanya*) from 21 to 30 degrees.
5. Jupiter is the lord of signs Sagittarius (*Dhan*) from 14 to 30 degrees and Pisces from 1 to 30 degrees.
6. Venus is the lord of signs Taurus (*Vrikh*) from 1 to 30 degrees and Libra (Tula) from 11 to 30 degrees.
7. Saturn is the lord of signs Capricorn (*Makar*) from 21 to 30 degrees and Aquarius (*Kumbh*) from 1 to 30 degrees.
8. Rahu is the lord of sign Virgo (*Kanya*) from 1 to 30 degrees.
9. Ketu is the lord of sign Pisces (*Meen*) from 1 to 30 degrees.

Exaltation of Planets

1. Sun is exalted in Aries (Mesh).
2. Moon is exalted in Taurus (*Vrikh*).
3. Mars is exalted in Capricorn (Makar).
4. Mercury is exalted in Virgo (*Kanya*).
5. Jupiter is exalted in Cancer (*Karak*).
6. Venus is exalted in Pisces (*Meen*).
7. Saturn is exalted in Libra (Tula).
8. Rahu is exalted in Taurus and Gemini (*Vrikh* and *Mithun*).
9. Ketu is exalted in Scorpio and Sagittarius (V*rishchak* and Sagittarius).

Peak Strength (*Mool-Trikon*) of Planets

1. Sun is in its *Mool-Trikon* in sign Leo (*Sinh*) from 1 to 20 degrees.
2. Moon is in its *Mool-Trikon* in Taurus (*Vrikh*) from 4 to 30 degrees.
3. Mars is in its *Mool-Trikon* in Aries (Mesh) from 1 to 18 degrees.

4. Mercury is in its *Mool-Trikon* in Virgo (*Kanya*) from 1 to 15 degrees.
5. Jupiter is on its *Mool-Trikon* in Sagittarius (*Dhan*) from 1to 13 degrees.
6. Venus is in its *Mool-Trikon* in Libra (Tula) from 1 to 10 degrees.
7. Saturn is in its *Mool-Trikon* in Aquarius (*Kumbh*) from 1to 20 degrees.
8. Rahu is in its *Mool-Trikon* in Cancer (*Karak*).
9. Ketu is in its *Mool-Trikon* in Leo (*Sinh*).

Debilitation of Planets

A planet in debilitation (*Neech sthan*) is inimical, malefic and harmful.

1. Sun is debilitated in sign Libra (Tula) at 10 degrees.
2. Moon is debilitated in Scorpio (*Vrishchak*) at 3 degrees.
3. Mars is debilitated in Cancer (*Karak*) at 28 degrees.
4. Mercury is debilitated in Pisces (*Meen*) at 15 degrees.
5. Jupiter is debilitated in Capricorn (*Makar*) at 5 degrees.
6. Venus is debilitated in Virgo (*Kanya*) at 27 degrees.
7. Saturn is debilitated in Aries (Mesh) at 20 degrees.
8. Rahu is debilitated in Scorpio (V*rishchak*) and Sagittarius (*Dhan*) at 15 degrees.
9. Ketu is debilitated in Taurus (V*rikh*) and Gemini (*Mithun*) at 15 degrees.

Friendly Signs of Planets

1. Sun is said to be in a friendly sign in Cancer, Scorpio, Sagittarius and Pisces.
2. Moon is said to be in a friendly sign in Aries, Leo, Sagittarius and Pisces.

3. Mars is said to be in a friendly sign in Leo, Sagittarius and Pisces.
4. Mercury is said to be in a friendly sign in Taurus, Leo, Libra, Capricorn and Aquarius.
5. Jupiter is said to be in a friendly sign in Aries, Leo and Scorpion.
6. Venus is said to be in a friendly sign in Gemini, Capricorn and Aquarius.
7. Saturn is said to be in a friendly sign in Taurus, Gemini and Virgo.
8. Rahu is said to be in a friendly sign in Virgo, Libra, Capricorn and Aquarius.
9. Ketu is said to be in a friendly sign in Virgo, Libra, Capricorn and Aquarius.

A planet in a friendly sign is usually favourable and helpful to the person.

Inimical Signs of Planets

1. The signs Taurus, Libra and Aquarius are inimical to planet Sun.
2. The signs Libra, Capricorn and Aquarius are inimical to Moon.
3. The sign Aquarius is inimical to Mars.
4. The sign Cancer is inimical to Mercury.
5. The signs Taurus, Libra and Aquarius are inimical to Jupiter.
6. The signs Leo and Sagittarius are inimical to Venus.
7. The signs Cancer, Leo, Scorpio, Sagittarius and Pisces are inimical to Saturn.
8. The signs Aries, Cancer, Leo and Pisces are inimical to Rahu.
9. The signs Aries, Cancer, Leo and Pisces are inimical to Ketu.

As the term "inimical" suggests, planets in their inimical signs exert a negative and harmful effect on the person.

Neutral Signs of Planets

1. Sun is said to be neutral in signs Gemini and Virgo.
2. Moon is said to be neutral in signs Gemini and Virgo
3. Mars is said to be neutral in signs in Taurus, Gemini, Virgo and Libra.
4. Mercury is said to be neutral in signs Aries, Scorpio and Sagittarius.
5. Jupiter is said to be neutral in Gemini and Virgo.
6. Venus is said to be neutral in Aries, Cancer and Scorpio.
7. Planets Saturn, Rahu and Ketu are not neutral in any sign.

As the term neutral suggests, planet in a neutral sign is neither beneficial nor harmful to the person.

Table showing 9 planets with their signs of lordship, their exalted signs, their signs of debilitation, friendly signs, inimical signs and neutral signs.

Planets	Signs of lordship	Sign of exaltation	Sign of Debilitation	Friendly signs	Inimical signs	Neutral signs
Sun	Leo(5)	Aries(1)	Libra(7)	Cancer, Scorpio, Sagittarius and Pisces (4, 8,9 and12)	Taurus, Libra and Aquarius(2,7 and 11)	Gemini and Virgo(3and 6)
Moon	Cancer(4)	Taurus(2)	Scorpio(8)	Aries, Leo, Sagittarius and Pisces(1, 5,9and12)	Libra, Capricorn and Aquarius(7, 10and11)	Gemini and Virgo(3and 6)

Mars	Aries and Scorpio(1 and 8)	Capricorn(10)	Cancer(4)	Leo, Sagittarius and Pisces(5, 9 and 12)	Aquarius(11)	Taurus, Gemini, Virgo and Libra(2,3,6 and 7)
Mercury	Gemini(3)	Virgo(6)	Pisces(12)	Taurus, Leo, Libra, Capricorn, Aquarius (2, 5,7,10,11)	Cancer(4)	Aries, Scorpio, Sagittarius (1, 8 and 9)
Jupiter	Sagittarius, Pisces(9, 12)	Cancer(4)	Capricorn (10)	Arises, Leo, Scorpion(1, 5 and 8)	Taurus, Libra, Aquarius(2, 7,11)	Gemini and Virgo(3 and, 6)
Venus	Taurus, Libra(2,7)	Pisces(12)	Virgo(6)	Gemini, Capricorn, Aquarius(3, 10 and 11)	Leo, Sagittarius(5 and 9)	Aries, Cancer and Scorpio(1,4 and 8)

Saturn	Capricorn, Aquarius(10 and 11)	Libra(7)	Aries(1)	Taurus, Gemini, Virgo(2,3 and 6)	Cancer, Leo, Scorpio, Sagittarius, Pisces(4,5,8,9 and 12, 9,12)
Rahu		Taurus, Gemini(2 and 3)	Scorpio, Sagittarius(8 and 9)	Virgo, Libra, Capricorn, Aquarius (6, 7,10, 11)	Aries, Cancer, Leo, Pisces(1,4,5 and 12)
Ketu		Scorpio, Sagittarius(8 and 9)	Taurus, Gemini (2 and 3)	Virgo, Libra, Capricorn, Aquarius(6,7,10,11)	Aries, Cancer, Leo, Pisces(1,4,5,12)

Effects of Planets Depending on Their Signs

In their *Mool-Trikon*/exaltation, specific planets exert the following effects:

1. Sun: It gives respect, fame, recognition, public acclaim/accolades, wealth and happiness.
2. Moon: It gives handsomeness/beauty, good fortune, wealth and happiness.
3. Mars: It gives average wealth, selfishness, meanness, philandering nature, anger and cruelty.
4. Mercury: It makes the person over-ambitious, doctor, soldier, businessman, university professor and scholar – honoured by the government and by the rich.
5. Jupiter: It makes the person highly popular, respected, famous – given to good things of life – devoted to gods and finds happiness in life.
6. Venus: It gives a person landed property, popularity among the members of opposite sex and many awards, prizes, titles and honours.
7. Saturn: It makes a person very brave, courageous, commander of armed forces, defence research scientist, a pilot etc., and devoted to duty.
8. Rahu: It makes the person greedy, talkative and wealthy.
9. Ketu: It gives courage, ability to engage in secretive activities, patience and capacity to bear hardship.

In their own signs, planets exert the following effects:

1. Sun: It gives physical beauty, wealth, good things of life, happiness, lust and proclivity to sexual affairs.
2. Moon: It gives the person handsomeness, an impressive personality, fortitude, wealth, physical and mental strength.
3. Mars: It makes a person an agriculturist, a farmer; usually brave, strong and famous.

4. Mercury: It gives knowledge of scriptures and makes one scholarly with many publications.
5. Jupiter: It gives one love of literature, knowledge of scriptures; could probably make one a physician and one is usually happy.
6. Venus: It makes one highly intellectual with independent views: also makes one rich, virtuous and scholarly.
7. Saturn: Makes a person short-tempered; person has capacity for hard work and ability to bear hardships.
8. Rahu: It makes a person fortunate, famous and good looking.
9. Ketu: Gives capacity for secretive activities and for withstanding hardships; it confers thoughtfulness and forbearance.

In their friendly signs, the planets exert the following effects:

1. Sun: Makes one charitable, famous, fortunate and adept in inter-personal relationships.
2. Moon: Makes one virtuous, wealthy and happy.
3. Mars: Makes one wealthy and fond of friends.
4. Mercury: Makes one crafty, dextrous, a practical joker, a comedian and gives one knowledge of scriptures.
5. Jupiter: Makes one wise, happy and progressive.
6. Venus: Makes one happy and virtuous with a large family.
7. Saturn: Makes one affectionate, rich, happy and prepared to accept food from others.
8. Rahu and 9. Ketu: Effects are similar to those of Saturn in a friendly sign.

Strength of Planets

General Features:

1. Sun and Moon are regarded as kings or rulers. Mercury is a prince; Mars is commander-in-chief; Venus and Jupiter are Ministers, and Saturn is a Server. To the extent and degree to which a particular planet affects a person's horoscope and life, it lends its own individual character to the person. For instance, if Sun or Moon is the dominant planet in a person's horoscope, that person would have the disposition of a king or ruler.

Particular Features:

Strength of a planet depends on six factors. These are:

1. **Placement Power (*sthan bal*):** This power depends on the house and the sign in which a planet is placed in the horoscope chart– whether it is exalted, in its Mool-Trikon or in its own sign, in a friendly sign, in an inimical sign or in the sign of its debilitation. The above stated order represents the descending order of strength of a planet. Thus a planet is most powerful in its exalted sign, next down in strength in its *Mool-Trikon*, next down the line is its placement in its own sign, next in descending order of strength is its placement in its inimical sign, and it is weakest in the sign of its debilitation. For example, the strength of planet Sun in descending order would be in sign Aries (1) where it is exalted, then in sign Leo (5) from 1 to 20 degrees where it is in its *Mool-Trikon*, next would be in its own sign Leo (5) from 21 to 30 degrees, next would be in Capricorn (10) where it is in an inimical sign and lastly it would be weakest in the sign of its debilitation which is Libra (7).

2. **Direction Power (*dig bal*):** 1st house represents East, 4th house is North, 7th house is West and 10th house is South.

    It was mentioned earlier that a horoscope has 4 squares/rectangles and these are called *Kendras* which means Centres and 8 triangles. The *Kendras* are more important than the other houses. Among the *Kendras*, 1st house is more important than the other 3 Kendras; in fact, the 1st house, also called Ascendant or Lagan is the most important house in the horoscope chart. Thus, any planet placed in the 1st house is more powerful as compared to its strength in other houses. Of the other 3 Kendras, 10th house is more important than 4th house and 7th house; 4th and 7th houses are of equal importance. 5th house and 9th house are Trikons and are next in importance to Kendras.

    Mercury and Jupiter are powerful in 1st house.
    Moon and Venus are powerful in 4th house.
    Saturn is powerful in 7th house.
    Sun and Mars are powerful in 10th house.

3. **Diurnal/Nocturnal Power:**

    If a person is born during night, Moon, Saturn and Mars are powerful in his/her horoscope.
    (b) If a person is born during daytime, Sun, Mercury and Venus are powerful in his/her horoscope.
    (c) Jupiter is equally powerful regardless of whether a person is born during daytime or during night.

4. **Innate Power (*naisargik bal*):**

    Mars is said to be more powerful than Saturn; Mercury is more powerful than Mars; Jupiter is more powerful than Mercury; Venus is more powerful than Jupiter; Moon is more powerful than Venus, and Sun is more powerful than Moon.

5. **Derivative Power (*cheshta bal*):**
   Sun and Moon are said to be more powerful in all the six signs extending from Capricorn (10) to Gemini (3), i.e., in signs 10, 11, 12, 1, 2 and 3.
   Venus and Saturn derive strength when they are in conjunction with Moon.
6. **Power Derived from Aspect (*drig bal*):**
   Malefic planets lose their malefic effect when aspected by a benefic planet and derive strength from the benefic planet.
7. **Power determined by their zodiacal sign:**
   Strength of a planet depends on the house of the horoscope which it occupies and on the zodiacal sign of that house.
   (a) A planet in the sign of its rulership/lordship exerts a very powerful influence on the life of that person.
   (b) A planet occupying its exalted sign is most powerful.
   (c) A planet in its *Mool-Trikon* is extremely powerful.
   (d) A planet occupying a friendly sign is quite powerful.
   (e) A planet placed in a debilitated sign is very weak and positively harmful to the person.
   (f) A planet in its inimical sign is quite harmful to the individual.
   (g) A planet in a neutral sign is neither helpful nor harmful.

Aspects of Planets (Drishti)

A planet has the power or ability to look at the other houses of the horoscope chart from where it is positioned with varying degrees of clarity and acuity of vision. This is known as the "aspect" of the planet or *drishti* in Sanskrit. The full vision or full aspect of a planet is described to consist of 4 *"charnas"* or parts whereas the partial aspect may consist of 1 to 3 *charnas*.

General Rules of Aspects of Planets:

1. Every planet aspects the 7th house from the house of its placement with full strength, i.e., with 4 *charnas*. For the purpose of determining the aspect of a planet, the counting is started from the house where the planet is located in a chart. For example, if planet Sun is located in House No. IV, the first house for the purpose of finding out its aspect/*drishti* would be taken as House No. IV itself and the 7th house from that house would be House No. X. Thus, one can say that Sun which is located in 4th house in the horoscope would aspect 10th house of the horoscope with its full strength or 4 *charnas*.
2. Every planet aspects the 4th and 10th house from it with 3 *charnas*.
3. Evert planet aspects the 5th and 9th house from it with 2 *charnas*, i.e. with half its full strength.
4. Every planet aspects the 3rd and 6th house from it with one *charna*, i.e., one-fourth of full strength.

Special Aspects of Planets:

In addition to the general rules stated above, special aspects of some specific planets are given as under:

1. Mars fully aspects the 4th and the 8th house from it, i.e. with 4 *charnas*.
2. Jupiter fully aspects the 5th and the 9th house from it.
3. Saturn fully aspects the 3rd and 10th house from it.
4. Rahu and Ketu fully aspect the 5th, 7th, 9th and 12th house from them.
5. Rahu and Ketu aspect 3rd and 6th house from them with 1charna, and 2nd and 10th house with 2 *charnas*.

The above points are being illustrated by drawings given on the next page.

However, for all practical purposes, usually, the full aspect (or *puran drishti*) of planets is usually taken into consideration for making predictions.

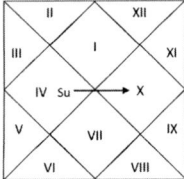

Diagram shows Sun in house IV fully aspecting House X with full drishti or 4 charnas.

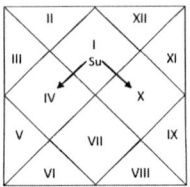

Diagram shows Sun in house I aspecting 4th and 10th houses from it with 3 charnas i.e. ¾ drishti.

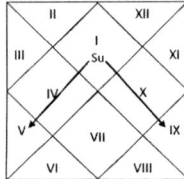

Diagram showing Sun in House I aspecting House numbers V and IX with 2 charnas or half drishti

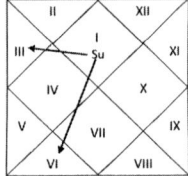

Diagram showing Sun in House I aspecting Houses III and VI with one charna or one-fourth drishti.

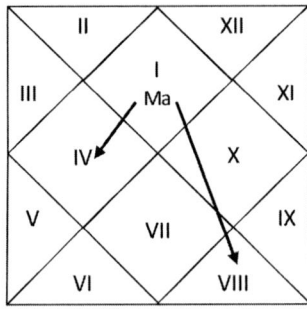

Diagram shows Mars in house I having its full special aspects on houses IV and VIII with 4 charnas i.e. full drishti

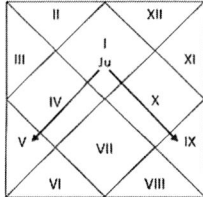

Diagram shows Jupiter in house I fully aspecting houses V and IX with 4 charnas, i.e. full drishti.

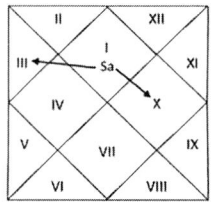

Diagram shows Saturn in house I aspecting fully houses III and X with 4 charnas or full drishti.

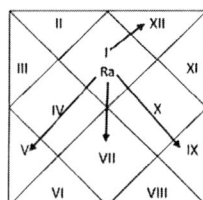

Diagram shows Rahu in house I aspecting houses V, VII, IX and XII with full drishti. The same applies equally to ketu.

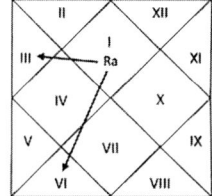

Diagram shows Rahu in house I aspecting houses III and VI with 1 charna, i.e. ¼ of full drishti. The same applies to ketu.

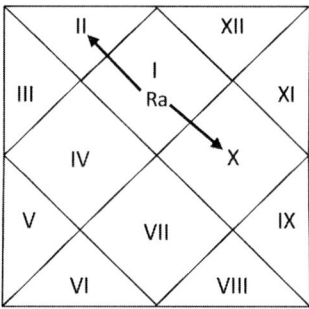

Diagram shows Rahu in house I aspecting houses II and X with 2 charnas, i.e. ½ of full drishti. The same applies equally to ketu.

Chapter II
Horoscope Chart

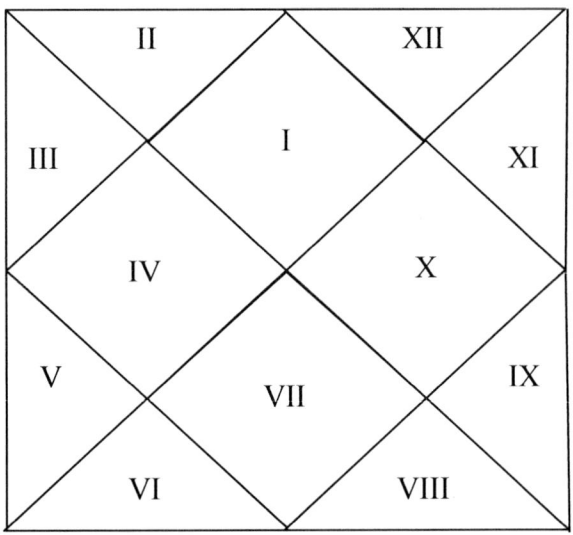

Heavenly space around the earth is like a sphere and encompasses 360 degrees like any other circle. In Indian astrology, this space is represented as a rectangle or a square and is called a horoscope chart. A horoscope chart consists of 12 houses and each house comprises 30 degrees. Above diagram depicts these twelve houses. It may be noted that there are 4 squares/rectangles and 8 triangles in a horoscope chart. The squares are called *Kendras*[*] and are considered more important than other houses in the matter of making

---

[*]Kendra means "Centre" in Sanskrit

predictions. The topmost square/rectangle in the chart is named as 1st house or ascendant and is the most important house in a horoscope and is also known as *"lagna"*. The remaining eleven houses are numbered one after another in a sequence in an anticlockwise manner shown in the diagram. Thus, taking the topmost square/rectangle as House No.1, one can work out the number of the succeeding eleven houses in an anticlockwise sequence as depicted in the above diagram.

In this book, wherever necessary, the house numbers would be shown in Latin numerals and the twelve zodiacal signs would be shown in Arabic numerals in order to avoid any confusion between the two.

The broad functions/portfolios of the twelve houses of a horoscope chart are as under:

12 Houses and Their Portfolio

House Number	Functions and Portfolios
I	Physical build, constitution, strength, appearance of a person; his intelligence, potential, personality, capacity, overall happiness, achievements, reputation and temperament.
II	One's wealth, bank balance, power of speech, eyes, titles, ancestry, clan, subsidiary business interests etc.
III	One's valour, courage, stamina, drive, perseverance; one's brothers and sisters; one's ears, arms and short journeys.
IV	One's house, landed property, vehicles of transport, one's mother, one's friends, one's heart, emotions and happiness

V	One's intelligence, education, one's children, power of speech, reputation, fame, administrative acumen and windfalls.
VI	One's enemies, illnesses, losses, doubts, litigations, fear of drowning, one's loans and debts, snake-bites, poisoning etc.
VII	One's marriage, spouse, relationship with partner, subsidiary business interests, partnerships, genital organs, public relations etc.
VIII	Longevity, span of life, cause of death, mental anxieties, obstacles in life, secrecy and interests in espionage, elusive nature, interests in occult sciences and archaeology, one's secret wealth, one's in-laws, likelihood of suffering a fracture or undergoing surgical operations etc.
IX	One's fortune, interest in religion, spiritual inclination, pilgrimages, happiness and support from father, windfalls, short journeys by air etc.
X	One's profession, occupation, business, connection with government, fame, public standing, reputation, social influence, authority, leadership qualities, relationship with father etc.
XI	One's regular income, salary, gain and profit, luxuries, good acts, ownership of vehicles of transport,

	one's wealth, possession of precious stones etc.
XII	One's losses, expenses, worries and anxieties, stay in foreign countries, bad habits, punishment, long travels by sea and air, charity etc.

Horoscope means a horoscope chart.

Horoscope Charts

Heavenly space around the earth is like a sphere and encompasses 360 degrees like any other circle.

Horoscope chart diagrammatically represents that space in the form of a rectangle or a square. There are 12 houses in a horoscope chart. Each house has 30 degrees. These twelve houses are named and numbered in an ascending manner anticlockwise.

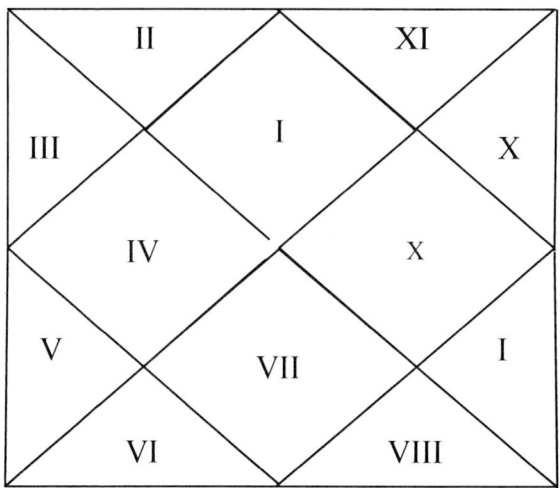

It may be noted that there are 4 squares and 8 triangles in the figure. The topmost square or rectangle is numbered as 1st house. It is also called ascendant or lagan. The four squares are called *Kendras* or the prominent houses in a horoscope; of these, the 1st house or the ascendant/*lagna* is the most important house in a horoscope chart. The remaining houses are numbered sequentially one after another in anticlockwise manner starting from 1st house.

How to Prepare a Horoscope Chart

Horoscope chart of a person is prepared according to date, time and place of his/her birth. Two things are required for this purpose:

 a) Finding the sign of ascendant (*Lagan Spasht*): There is a section in the later pages of a *Panchang* or *Jantri* entitled *"Lagan Sarni"*. One can find out the "lagan" or ascendant by referring to this page in the *Panchang/Jantri*. Once, the sign of the ascendant is found out, the signs of the other houses get automatically worked out in a sequential manner.
 b) Precise degrees of planets: Another section in the *Panchang* or *Jantri* called *"Niryam graha spashta prate* 5.30 am". By referring to this page, one can find out the location and degrees of the 9 planets in the horoscope.

The horoscope chart is usually prepared by a professional astrologer trained in calculations of the movement of planets or by accessing a computer with appropriate software.

When preparing a horoscope of a person, several charts are prepared. These are:

1. Basic Horoscope or *Janamangam*/birth chart/*Janam kundli*. For example, if a child is born in *Jalandar* (Punjab, India) on Friday, 10th May 2002 at 2.00 PM, a reference to Lagan *Sarni* in *Jantri* would show that his ascendant is Leo (*Sinh*). Placement of the planets is worked out by referring to *"Niyam graha spashta prate"*. Horoscope chart of this child would read as:

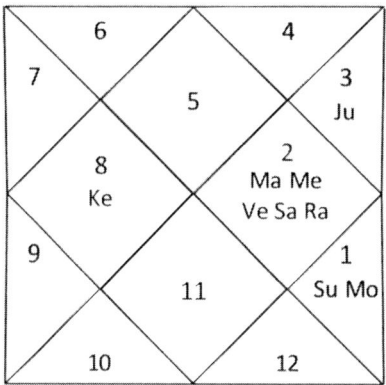

Janam Kundli(JK) of a child born
on 10/05/2002 at 2.PM in
Jalandhar, Punjab, India.

The chart shows the ascendant (1st house) to have sign 5 in it, and we know that sign 5 stands for Leo; the other houses get their signs automatically assigned to them in a sequential manner. Further, we find that the planet Ketu is placed in the 4th house in sign 8 (Scorpio); Sun and Moon are placed in house number IX in sign 1(Aries). Also, planets Mars, Mercury, Venus, Saturn and Rahu are located in house number X in sign 2 (Taurus) while planet Jupiter is located in XIth house in sign 3 (Gemini).

This horoscope chart is called *Janamangam/Janam* (lagan) *Kundli*.

This is the basic horoscope chart of a person and it gives a very good general idea about the person.

Names of Various Horoscope Charts and Their Relative Importance in Prediction

A professional astrologer normally prepares several other charts in addition to *Janamangam*. The names of horoscope charts usually prepared for a person are:

1. *Janam Kundli* or *Janamangam*. This is the basic chart.
2. *Chander Kundli*: This is a chart with planet Moon in the ascendant or the 1st house.
3. *Surya Kundli*: This chart is prepared showing planet Sun in the ascendant.
4. *Hora Chakra*: This chart tells mainly about the wealth of a person.
5. *Saptansh*: This chart tells mainly about the children of a person.
6. *Navamsh*: This chart is a more elaborate, detailed and magnified view of the birth chart and is taken into account in making any prediction about a person. It is particularly important in predicting about the spouse, profession and overall standing and status of a person.
7. *Dreshkon*
8. *Dwadshansh*
9. *Trishansh*
10. *Gochar*: This chart shows the current position of the planets in the heavenly space. It is helpful in answering any questions at any given point in time in relation to a person or for casting what is called, "*Prashan Kundli*".

For all practical purposes, the *Janam Kundli, Chander Kundli, Navamsh* and *Gochar* are the ones which are mainly taken into consideration for making predictions or "*phaladesh*".

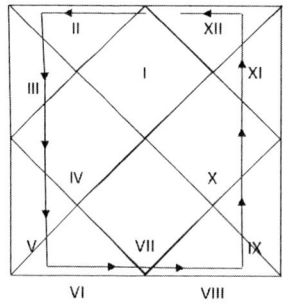
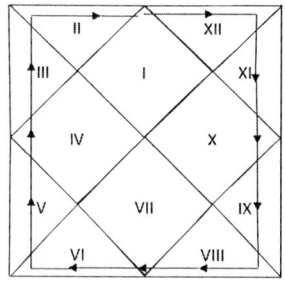

Diagram showing forward anticlockwise movements of planets in a horoscope chart.

Diagram depicting retrograde clockwise movements of planets in a horoscope chart.

Movement of Planets in a Horoscope Chart

The horoscope chart of a person is prepared according to the time, date and place of birth of a person. Two parameters are required for this purpose.

a) Ascendant/*lagna*/1st house: This is determined by referring to what is called "Lagan Sarni", which is located in the later pages of an Indian almanac/*Panchang* or *Jantri*.
b) Precise degrees and signs of planets. This is found out by referring to a section of Indian almanac or *Panchang* known as "*Niryan graha spashta prate* 5.30 am".

The horoscope chart is usually prepared by a professional astrologer or by a hobbyist having access to a computer with the requisite software.

Each planet moves 360 degrees in completing its one orbital cycle. The nine planets move through all the 12 houses of a horoscope chart in order to complete their full cycle of 360 degrees.

As stated earlier, each house of a horoscope chart comprises 30 degrees. A planet enters a house at 0 degree, completes 30 degrees of its journey in that house and then enters the next house at 0 degree. Thus a planet may occupy a position ranging from 0 degree to 30 degrees in a house at any given point in time and an Indian almanac or *Panchang* would indicate its exact degrees at that time.

Usually the movement of a planet is in a forward direction in the heavenly space and this is known as the "forward or prograde" movement of a planet. However, sometimes, the planet may move in a backward direction in the heavenly space and this is known as the "retrograde movement" of a planet.

Sun and Moon always move in a forward direction and Rahu and Ketu always move in a backward or retrograde direction. The other five planets, Mars, Mercury, Jupiter, Venus and Saturn, although usually moving in a forward direction, sometimes move in a retrograde direction. The duration of retrograde movement of any one of these five planets is clearly indicated in the almanac or *Panchang*.

The exact degree of placement of planets in the 12 houses of a horoscope chart depends on the time and place of birth of an individual. This is found out by referring to a section called "*lagan sarni*" in an Indian almanac or *Panchang*.

Retrograde movement of a planet

Retrograde movement of the five planets, namely, Mars, Mercury, Jupiter, Venus and Saturn, occurs from time to time in the heavenly space. This is for a variable period of time lasting from a few weeks to a few months; usually it is for a short period of time only but occasionally it may last for a few months. The duration of this retrograde movement is clearly indicated in Indian almanac or *Panchang*. After completion of its retrograde movement, the planet resumes its customary forward movement. The retrograde movement may take place within the same house where the planet is located at the start of this movement or the planet may even move back into a preceding house.

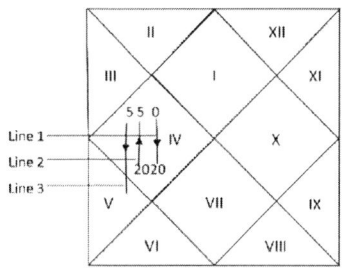 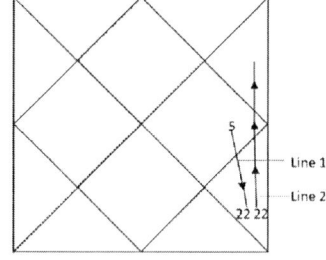

Explanation of Diagrams

Diagram on the left depicts the onset of retrograde movement of planet Venus in House No. IV when Venus had reached 20 degrees in that house by its forward movement (Line 1). During its retrograde movement lasting 2 weeks, it moved back to 5 degrees in that house (Line 2) and then resumed its usual forward movement (Line 3). This is an example to illustrate the retrograde movement of a planet.

Diagram on the right shows another situation depicting the retrograde movement of the same planet. Venus was located at 5 degrees in House No. X at the start of becoming retrograde. The retrograde movement continued for 17 days and it moved back into House No. IX and it kept moving backwards until it reached 22 degrees in that house (Line 1). Thereafter, Venus resumed its customary forward movement (Line 2).

Configuration of 30 Degrees in a House of a Horoscope Chart

The following simple points need to be understood in relation to the houses of a horoscope chart:

1. Each one of the twelve houses of a horoscope chart consists of 30 degrees.
2. When a forward moving planet enters a house in a horoscope chart, it does so at 0 degree and after moving through 30 degrees in that house, it completes its stay in that house and leaves that house to enter the next house at 0 degree.

3. When a retrograde planet enters a house, it does so at 30 degrees and moving backwards in that house, it leaves it at 0 degree to enter the next house at 30 degrees.

The above points are illustrated in the diagrams given below:

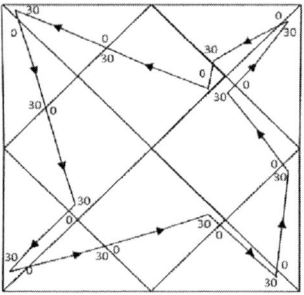 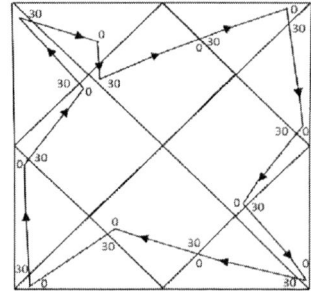

Figure on the left shows the configuration of 30 degrees in a horoscope chart in the twelve houses for forward movement of planets in it. The line drawing appears somewhat zigzag in an attempt to figuratively depict the layout of 0 to 30 degrees in each house. It may be noted that the forward movement is anticlockwise and it starts at 0 degree in a house and ends at 30 degrees.

Figure on the right shows figuratively the retrograde movement of a planet such as that of Rahu through the twelve houses of a horoscope. Rahu, as we know, always moves in a retrograde manner. It may be noted that when a retrograde planet enters a house, it does so at 30 degrees and completes its 30 degrees from 30 degrees to 0 degree to enter the next house at 30 degrees. Retrograde movement is clockwise.

Chapter III
Zodiacal Signs

The twelve zodiacal signs used in astrology have been mentioned earlier with their names and their signs ranging from 1to 12 (page 7).

A horoscope chart has twelve houses and each of these houses have one zodiacal sign in it. The zodiacal sign of 1st house or Ascendant is determined by the time and place of birth of a person. It is found out by referring to "*lagan sarni*" in Indian almanac or *Jantri**. For example, if the sign of 1st house is found out to be Scorpio (or 8) at the time of birth of a person, then a horoscope chart is drawn showing sign Scorpio (8) in the 1st house. The signs of the remaining eleven houses get automatically determined in a sequential manner. Thus, the sign of the 2nd house would be Sagittarius which is the sign next to Scorpio; the sign of 3rd house would be Capricorn which is next to Sagittarius; the sign of the 4th house would be Aquarius which is next to Capricorn and so on. Thus each of the twelve houses in a Chart gets a sign assigned to it serially in a sequential manner. It is important to remember that zodiacal sign is a distinct number and is not identical with the house number of a horoscope chart. For example, the zodiacal sign in house number I may be 6; then, for house number II, it would be sign 7; for house number Ill, it would be sign 8; for house number IV, it would be 9 and so on serially in a progressive manner in subsequent houses. Sign means zodiacal sign.

Jantri is the Indian almanac and is available in Hindi, Urdu, other regional languages of India.

Please note that the house numbers of horoscope are depicted by Roman numerals whereas the zodiacal signs are depicted in Arabic numerals in the above diagram.

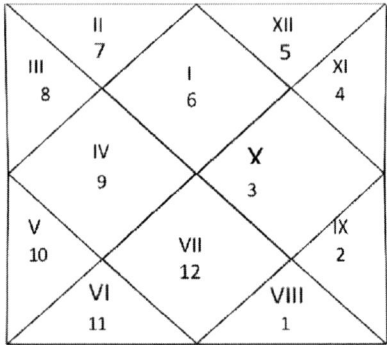

Diagram shows a horoscope chart drawn on the basis of date and place of birth of a person, where the "lagan sarni" showed that at the time of birth, the sign Virgo (6) was present in house I or ascendant. Once the sign of 1st house is known, the houses following house I, automatically get a sign assigned to them in a sequential manner.

Characteristics of Twelve Zodiacal Signs

1. Aries (*Mesh*): This sign is masculine, yellowish-red in colour, lord of Eastern direction, fiery, brave, generous, arrogant and connected with brain cells.
2. Taurus (*Vrikh*): This sign is feminine, fair in complexion, auspicious, loquacious, selfish, worldly-wise, intelligent, crafty and represents mouth and lips.
3. Gemini (*Mithun*): It is masculine, lord of West, airy in nature, extremely loquacious, studious, moderately fertile and represents shoulders and arms.
4. Cancer (*Karak*): It is feminine, lord of North, benign, extremely fertile, shy and modest, dedicated to worldly progress with ability to rise to occasion and represents kidneys.
5. Leo (*Sinh*): It is masculine, yellowish, lord of East, fiery in temper, healthy of body, of low fertility,

generous, independent, loves to travel and represents heart.
6. Virgo (*Kanya*): It is feminine, lord of South, of low fertility, attentive to its self-respect and prestige and represents abdomen.
7. Libra (*Tula*): It is masculine, dark in colour, lord of West, fond of acquiring knowledge, politically inclined, intellectual, go-getter and represents lower parts of the body.
8. Scorpio (*Vrishak*): It is feminine, lord of North, highly fertile, candid and straightforward, clean, determined, even stubborn and indicates genital parts.
9. Sagittarius (*Dhan*): It is masculine, golden in colour, lord of East, powerful during day time, of low fertility, of strong body, generous, upholder of traditions, authoritative and tells about legs and feet
10. Capricorn (*Makar*): This is feminine, lord of South, cold-blooded, hankering after very high positions and indicates feet and ankles.
11. Aquarius (*Kumbh*): This is masculine, lord of West, of moderate fertility, powerful during daytime, peaceful in temper, intellectual, religious, inventive and tells about the interior of abdomen.
12. Pisces (*Meen*): It is feminine, lord of North, powerful at night, generous, benevolent and philanthropic and tells about feet.

The above-described features are more noticeable when the sign is located in the ascendant/*kendra* and are slightly less conspicuous in other houses of horoscope.

Effects of Placement of Different Zodiacal Signs in 1st House or Ascendant

The presence of a zodiacal sign in the twelve houses of a horoscope chart is determined by the date, time and place of birth of a person. As mentioned earlier, the ascendant or the first house is the most important house in a chart. The zodiacal sign of the first house has a special characteristic effect on the nature, character and fortune of a person. This effect is independent of the placement of the planets in the chart. The predictive effects of the placement of different zodiacal signs in the ascendant or *lagan* is being taken up now.

1. A person with sign 1 or Aries in the first house tends to be slim, talkative, of a reddish complexion, hot-tempered, proud, restless, clever, religious, wise, generous, has a small family, not fond of opposite sex, fond of good things of life, is jewel of the family; onset of good fortune in life is 28th or 34th year of life.
2. Person with sign 2 or Taurus in the first house tends to have a fair or wheatish complexion, is lady-like in habits, is fond of self-decoration, sweet of tongue, may have long teeth and curly hair, has many talents and virtues, is supremely wise, intelligent, has a stable character, is brave and courageous with remarkable equipoise, demonstrates full strength in a fight, is famous, attentive to family, is argumentative and would have a long life.
3. Person with sign 3 or Gemini in the first house tends to be wheatish in complexion, may have a round face, have beautiful hair, is fond of music, dance and opposite sex, is witty, humorous, could be a comedian, is polite and sweet of tongue, excellent in inter-personal relations and an excellent messenger; would be generous, clever, enjoys good things of life, is close to the ruling administration, lives to a moderate age; would be happy in early life, unhappy in middle life and very happy in later life. Onset of good fortune is between 32 and 35 years of life.
4. Person with sign 4 or Cancer in the 1st house tends to have a fair complexion, is slim but has a strong build; is fond of sweet foods, of aquatic sports and persons of good character; is generous, polite, wise, clean, religious, a great soul; is stubborn but forgiving, tends to be a businessman, may have many daughters, is

wealthy, may have addictions; could be devious and procrastinating, capable of exhibiting spurts of aberrant behaviour and settles away from the place of birth. Rise of good fortune is 16 to 17 years of life.

5. Person with sign 5 or Leo in the 1st house tends to have a wheatish or earthly complexion, has long hands and feet, broad chest and broad shoulders, has a slim waist-line and is figure conscious, is non-vegetarian and fond of delicious food but is a sparse eater, has few sons, is extremely hard working, proud, arrogant, pleasure-seeking, given to good things of life, of sharp intellect, bold, immodest, not respectful of elders and seniors, fond of travelling, has ostentatious life-style, is a show-off, fond of horse riding, well-versed in arguments, aggressive, may know *Vedanta*, is generous and fond of looking after sadhus and saints, is happy in early life, unhappy in middle life and extremely happy in the last phase of life; rise of good fortune is 21st or 28th year of life.

6. A person born with sign Virgo (6) in the Ascendant is handsome, intellectual, has many children, is dominated by spouse, is timid, crafty, clever, gets a beautiful spouse, fond of sex, is specially gifted and talented, is always happy and cheerful, is fond of self-decoration, has big eyes, is fat, is sweet of tongue, uses few words, is hostile to brothers, interested in mathematics and religion, is serious-minded, is fond of travelling, has fine manners and delicate habits, has an elusive personality, covers up his/her thoughts or disguises them, keeps his cards close to his/her chest. He or she is happy in early life, has average happiness in middle life and is unhappy in the last phase of life. Rise of fortune is between 24th and 26th year of life.

7. A person born with sign Libra (7) in Ascendant has a fair complexion, may have a flabby body and a thick nose. He or she is bestowed with many talents and gifts of nature, is extremely capable in his/her chosen profession, is wealthy, famous and is the shining

jewel of the family. He/She is truthful, honoured by the government, religiously devout person and very helpful to others. He or she is philanthropic, performer of good and noble deeds, loves to perform pilgrimages, is a very affectionate person, interested in astrology and is not greedy. He/she is unhappy in early life, happy in middle life and very busy and happy in later life. Rise of good fortune is 31st to 32nd year.

8. A person born with sign Scorpio (8) in the Ascendant is extremely brave, highly intellectual, has a flawless character, possesses high qualifications, is short-tempered and is honoured by the government. He/she has many virtues and talents and has knowledge of literature and scriptures. He/she is crafty, clever, imposter, could at times tell a lie and occasionally have a low and mean mentality. He/she is a good perceiver of other person's mind and could sometimes show an unpleasant behaviour. He/she is short and stout with round eyes, has a broad chest, is hostile to brother and could be an astrologer. He/she usually works as an employee. He/she is happy in early life and also in middle life. Rise of good fortune is 20th or 24th year of life.

9. A person born with sign Sagittarius (9) in the 1st house is reddish brown or yellowish in complexion, has a radiant personality and may have long teeth. He/she is very good in his work, is respectful to seniors and elders, is devoted to gods, is helpful to friends and is close to government. He/she is a very knowledgeable person, knows many arts and possesses many talents, is committed to truth, is very wise and handsome. He is performer of good and noble deeds and is devoted to spouse. He/she has a remarkably good nature, is wealthy and enjoys good things and comforts of life. He/she could be a poet, an author or in business, loves travelling, is extremely hard working and has a small family. He/she is easily

won over by love and affection. He/she is happy in early life, has average happiness in middle life and is full of good things, comforts and wealth in later life. Rise of good fortune is 22nd or 23rd year of life.

10. A person born with sign Capricorn (10) in Ascendant is tall, contented, quick-tempered, always endeavouring, has big eyes and is happy go lucky. He/she is clever, greedy, a bit of a knave and is extravagant and could occasionally be mean. He/she is fond of opposite sex, could be a poet and is usually devoid of modesty. He/she is happy in early life and remains very happy from 32 years onwards till the end of life and enjoys a long life.

11. A person born with Aquarius sign (11) in Ascendant tends to be talkative, uses a lot of water, has a beautiful spouse and tends to strike friendship with big personalities and is popular and is loved by friends. He/she is extremely busy, has a flickering mind and tends to be untruthful and a bit of an imposter. He/she has an impressive personality, has a thick neck, a bald head and prefers company of opposite sex. He is proud, jealous, harbours inimical feelings, opposes brothers and is unhappy in early life. He is happy in middle life and enjoys landed property, houses, wealth and other good things in later life.

12. A person with Pisces sign (12) in the Ascendant tends to be good at aquatic sports, is polite, is beloved of spouse and is very speedy in movements and actions. He could be a distinguished Pundit, is clever, eats sparsely, has an unsteady mind, wears precious stones and could be a builder of many things including institutions.

Table showing sign numbers of twelve zodiacal signs and their lordship

Sign Number	Zodiacal Signs	Lordship
1	Aries	Mars
2	Taurus	Venus
3	Gemini	Mercury
4	Cancer	Moon
5	Leo	Sun
6	Virgo	Mercury
7	Libra	Venus
8	Scorpio	Mars
9	Sagittarius	Jupiter
10	Capricorn	Saturn
11	Aquarius	Saturn
12	Pisces	Jupiter

Chapter IV
Predictions

Effects of Placement of Lords of the Twelve Houses of Horoscope

Effects of the location of lord of 1st House (Ascendant or lagan) If lord of 1st house is located in:

1. 1st house itself, then the person would have a strong physique, good health and long life. His life would be like that of a king and he would own a lot of landed property.
2. If it is in the 2nd house, the person would be obese, strong, have a long life, would be very rich, would be spiritually inclined and own a lot of property.
3. If it is in 3rd house, the person would be strong, brave, would have highly placed and influential friends and would have lots of material possessions.
4. If it is in 4th house, the person would be a sparse eater, have a long life, would be devoted to parents, would earn money with help of his father, and would be rich, happy and highly respected.
5. If it is in 5th house, the person would be generous, have a long life, would be religious, famous, rich and happy, would have abundance of material possessions and have outstanding sons.
6. If it is in 6th house, the person would be rich, strong, would perform high quality work, would own landed property, would be famous and live a happy life.

7. If it is in 7th house, the person would have impressive personality, his wife would be extremely beautiful and have a radiant personality; he would be very polite and possess high character. He may face some domestic problems.
8. If it is in 8th house, the person would have a long life, would be miserly and spendthrift. If the planet is malefic or is in conjunction with another malefic planet, then the person would be blind of one eye. If the planet is benefic or is in conjunction with a benefic planet, then the person would be good looking and gentle.
9. If it is in 9th house, the person would have a large family and an average number of friends. He would be a learned person, famous, happy and live an honourable and respectable life.
10. If it is in 10th house, the person would gain wealth and title from government, would be a learned person, gentle, devoted to parents and guru and would be famous.
11. If it is in 11th house, the person would have an impressive and attractive personality, would be renowned, would be blessed with sons, would be strong and have a long life. He would be rich and live a happy life.

12. If it is in 12th house, the person is likely to perform evil deeds, may have a mean mentality, may be controversial and arrogant and may live abroad.

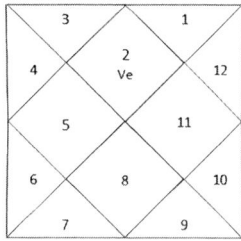

Horoscope chart showing lord of ascendant, Venus, located in 1st house in sign Taurus.

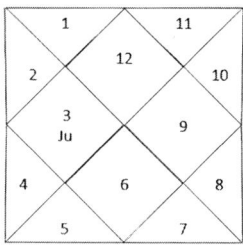

Chart showing lord of lagna (ascendant), Jupiter located in 4th house in sign Gemini.

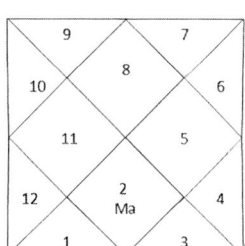

Chart showing lord of lagna (ascendant), Mars, located in 7th house in sign Taurus.

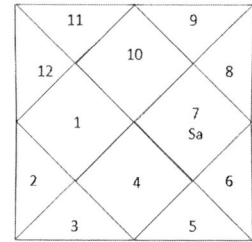

Chart showing lord of lagna Saturn, located in 10th house in sign Libra.

Effects of Location of Lord of 2nd House in the Horoscope

If lord of 2nd house is located in:

1. 1st house, the person is likely to be miserly and engaged in business. He would be rich, happy, and famous and enjoy good things of life and perform some good deeds.
2. 2nd house, the person makes his livelihood through business, is happy and famous, is excitable and has a proclivity for doing unpopular tasks.
3. 3rd house and if it is a "benefic" planet then the person likes to live with his brother; if it is "malefic" then the person is easily excitable and is opposed to the government of the day. If its lord is Mars, then the person is likely to be a thief.

4. 4th house and is "benefic", then the person gets benefited by his/her father, calls spade a spade, is generous and has a long life. If the lord is "malefic", then the person loses his/her mother at a young age.
5. 5th house, the person enjoys the money earned by his/her sons, is miserly, is unhappy and is adept and famous for carrying out difficult tasks.
6. 6th house, the person saves and hoards money and is an agriculturist. If the planet is malefic, the person has very little money.
7. 7th house, then the person has a wise spouse who is fond of sex and pleasures of life and hoards money. If it is a malefic planet, then the spouse is likely to be infertile.
8. 8th house, the person is likely to commit suicide, dissipates his own or other person's wealth, is poor and a fatalist.
9. 9th house and is "benefic", the person is a philanthropist and an impressive orator. If it is malefic, the person is controversial, critical of others and may be an exhibitionist or a mimic.
10. 10th house, the person is honoured and awarded land by the government. If it is a benefic planet, the person takes good care of his parents.
11. 11th house, the person makes his livelihood trading in birds, looks after a large number of persons and is famous.
12. 12th house, the person is poor. If the lord is benefic, then the person has a mixed fortune of gains and losses but is famous.

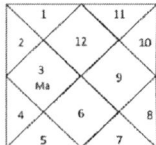

Horoscope showing lord of 2nd house Mars, placed in 4th house in sign Gemini.

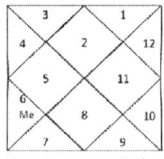

Chart showing lord of 2nd house, Mercury in 5th house in sign Virgo.

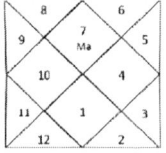

Chart showing lord of 2nd house, Mars located in 1st house in sign Libra.

Effects of Location of the Lord of 3rd House

If the lord of 3rd house is located in:

1. 1st house, the person is argumentative, fond of sex, inclined to serve others, has differences with own people, has evil-minded friends, is manoeuvring and quarrelsome.
2. 2nd house and is a malefic planet then the person has a short life, is poor and hostile to siblings. If it is a benefic planet then the person is rich and very powerful like a king.
3. 3rd house, the person is of medium strength, has many siblings and friends, is devoted to guru and gods and receives honour and awards from the government.
4. 4th house, the person enjoys the support of father and family, is opposed to mother and dissipates ancestral property
5. 5th house, the person is looked after by his sons or his brother's sons or by brothers, has a long life and is helpful to others.
6. 6th house, the person is prone to eye problems, profits from landed property, is opposed to brothers and is afflicted by some specific illness.
7. 7th house, the person is blessed with a lucky, good-natured and devoted spouse. If the planet is malefic, then the spouse may be in love with the person's sibling.
8. 8th house, the person is bereft of siblings. If it is a malefic planet, the person may be born devoid of a limb and may not live for more than 8 years.
9. 9th house and if it is a benefic planet, the person is highly educated and has great affection for siblings. If it is a malefic planet, then the person is hostile to siblings.
10. 10th house, the person is devoted to parents, has tremendous affection for siblings and is honoured by the government.

11. 11th house, the person has a large number of siblings, looks after siblings, is given to pleasures of life and is wealthy like a king.
12. 12th house, the person is opposed to friends and siblings, is indolent and is unemployed.

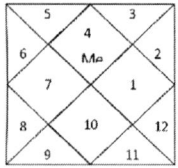 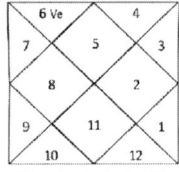 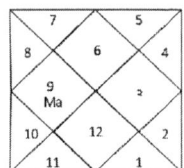

Chart showing lord of 3rd house, Mercury, in 1st house in sign Cancer.

Chart showing lord of 3rd house, Venus, in 2nd house in sign Virgo.

Chart showing lord of 3rd house, Mars, in 4th house in sign Sagittarius.

Effects of Placement of Lord of 4th House in the Horoscope

If the lord of 4th house is located in:

1. 1st house, the person likes his/her father, is opposed to mother's family and earns fame from the name of his/her father.
2. 2nd house and is malefic, the person is opposed to his/her father but if it is benefic, then he takes care of his/her father and the father enjoys the wealth earned by the person.
3. 3rd house, the person causes a lot of unhappiness to parents, is opposed to other persons and is harmful to father's siblings.
4. 4th house, the person enjoys landed property, owns a big house and a number of vehicles. He gives happiness to parents, is devoutly religious, rich, happy and famous.
5. 5th house, the person enjoys help and happiness from father, has a long life, performs good actions, is famous, is blessed with many sons and enjoys happiness from them.

6. 6th house and is benefic, the person saves and hoards money; if the planet is malefic, the person destroys the wealth of mother and is critical of father.
7. 7th house and is benefic, the person's wife takes care of his parents. If it is malefic, the person's wife does not look after his parents. If the planet is Mars or Venus, then his wife is endowed with many talents.
8. 8th house, the person is cruel in nature, is poor and in ill health, given to bad actions and wishes to die all the time.
9. 9th house, the person lives separately from his father, is very knowledgeable, is devoted to religion but does not fulfil the expectations of father.
10. 10th house and is benefic, then the person is helpful to others. If it is malefic, then his father leaves his mother and takes another woman.
11. 11th house, the person is devoted to father performs good deeds, is healthy and enjoys a long life.
12. 12th house, the person loses his father at a young age or he lives abroad. If it is malefic, the person may be illegitimate, i.e. not the offspring of his legal father.

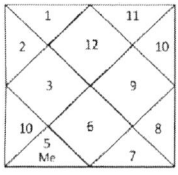
Chart showing lord of 4th house, Mercury, in 6th house in sign Leo.

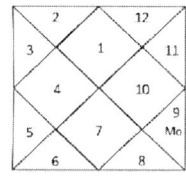
Chart showing lord of 4th house, Moon, in 9th house in sign Sagittarius.

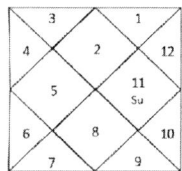
Chart showing lord of 4th house, Sun, in 10th house in sign Aquarius.

Effects of Placement of Lord of Fifth House

If the lord of 5th house is located in:

1. 1st house, the person has few children, performs good deeds, is well versed in literature and is famous.
2. 2nd house and is benefic, the person is rich. If the planet is malefic, the person is poor.
3. 3rd house, the person is sweet of tongue, enjoys a much wider fame than his siblings and looks after collateral family members.
4. 4th house, the person adopts the profession of his father, is looked after by his father and is devoted to his mother. If it is a malefic planet, the person is opposed to his parents.
5. 5th house, the person is wise, gifted, self-conscious of his talents and has many children.
   He is influential and is outstanding among the famous persons.
6. 6th house, the person is devoid of honour, is ill, poor and has many enemies. If it is a malefic planet, the negative effects are worse.
7. 7th house, the person is blessed with handsome sons, is of gentle nature, is devoted to gods and guru and his wife is of gentle nature.
8. 8th house, the person is devoid of education and has a harsh tongue. His wife is cruel in nature and so are his brothers and sons.
9. 9th house, the person is a poet, musician, actor or a dancer, is very handsome, is highly educated and wise and is honoured by the government.
10. 10th house, the person is close to the government and works for the government, performs good deeds, gives happiness to mother and is outstanding among good persons.
11. 11th house, the person is endowed with many sons, is truthful, brave, has knowledge of music and arts and lives a happy life.

12. 12th house and is malefic, then the person is devoid of children. If it is a benefic planet, then he has male children and lives abroad.

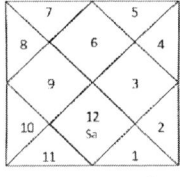
Chart showing lord of 5th house, Saturn, in 7th house in sign Pisces.

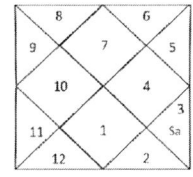
Chart showing lord of 5th house, Saturn, in 9th house in sign Gemini.

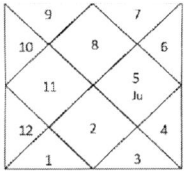
Chart showing lord of 5th house, Jupiter, in 10th house in sign Leo.

Effect of Placement of Lord of Sixth House

If lord of 6th house is placed in:

1. 1st house, the person is healthy and strong and conquers his/her enemies, has independent views, is talkative, rich, likely to trouble collateral relatives and has expectations from many persons.
2. 2nd house, the person is clever, poor in health, amasses lot of money, lives in a good house, is famous, is jealous, has a bad nature and destroys the wealth of his friends.
3. 3rd house, the person causes trouble to others, is cruel to one's dependents and suffers personally from quarrels and fights.
4. 4th house, the person gains landed property; he is opposed to his father and his father suffers a protracted illness.
5. 5th house and if it is a benefic planet, he has average relations with his father but he is hostile to others and is deceitful. If it is a malefic planet, there is hostility between father and son and the son becomes the cause of death of his father.
6. 6th house, the person is free from disease and enemies. He/she is miserly and lives in a house

somewhat below his/her status. He/she has a lot of patience and has a happy life.

7. 7th house, – is benefic, then his wife is well-disposed towards him but is infertile or prone to abortions and miscarriages. If the planet is malefic, his wife is cruel and hostile and causes him a lot of unhappiness.

8. 8th house and is Saturn, then the person dies from malabsorption, if it is Mars then he dies from snake-bite, if it is Mercury then he suffers from poisoning, if it is Moon then he dies from a childhood disease, if it is Sun then he dies from an attack by a lion, if it is Jupiter then he dies from some stupid action and if it is Venus then he dies from an eye illness.

9. 9th house and if it is malefic, then the person is lame, hostile to brothers and unbeliever in scriptures and *shastras*; if it is benign, then none of these negative effects are observed.

10. 10th house and if it is benefic, then the person looks after his father but is hostile to other members of the family; if malefic, then he has a cruel nature and is hostile to mother.

11. 11th house and if it is benefic, then he gains from quadrupeds or animals but is robbed of his money by thieves; if malefic, then the person is killed by his enemies.

12. 12th house, he earns money in foreign countries and is fatalist but suffers losses on account of animals.

Chart showing lord of 6th house, Jupiter in 10th house in sign Cancer.

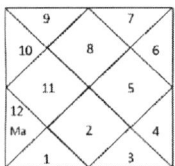
Chart showing lord of 6th house, mars, in 5th house in sign Pisces.

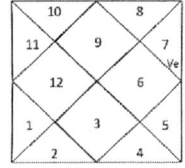
Chart showing lord of 6th house, Venus, in 11th house in sign Libra.

Effects of Placement of Lord of Seventh House

If the lord of 7th house is located in the:

1. 1st house, the person is very fond of his wife, is handsome and may have interest in other ladies as well.
2. 2nd house, his wife is interested in having a male issue and is helpful to the person; she may be cruel. Person himself is fond of loneliness.
3. 3rd house, the person is strong-willed, fond of siblings but is personally unhappy. If it is a malefic planet, his wife may be in love with his younger brother or his friends.
4. 4th house, the person is of unsteady nature and fond of the enemies of his father. His father is harsh in tongue. His wife spends a lot of time in her parent's house.
5. 5th house, the person has good fortune, has many sons, is courageous and believes in the present. His wife is looked after by his son.
6. 6th house, the person is hostile to his wife and his wife may suffer from some chronic illness. If it is a malefic planet, he may die soon after his marriage.
7. 7th house, the person has long life, has an impressive personality, is good-natured, is popular and has many friends.
8. 8th house, the person does not marry and spends his time with prostitutes and is beset with anxieties and unhappiness.
9. 9th house, the person is gentle and influential and has a gentle wife. If it is a malefic planet, he may be impotent and ugly. If the planet is aspected by the lord of 1st house then the person has special skills in diplomacy.
10. 10th house, the person is deceitful and is rebellious against the government. If it is a malefic planet, then he is miserable and under the influence of enemies.

11. 11th house, then the person's wife is beautiful, extremely good tempered and devoted.
12. 12th house, then his wife is fond of his brothers and friends. She is of unsteady nature, may be fond of bad persons and spends her time away from her husband.

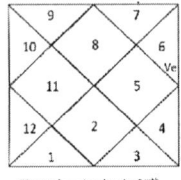

Chart showing lord of 7th house, Venus, in 11th house in sign Virgo.

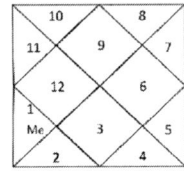

Chart showing lord of 7th house, Mercury, in 5th house in sign Aries.

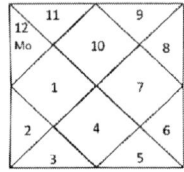

Chart showing lord of 7th house, Moon, in 3rd house in sign Pisces.

Effects of Placement of Lord of 8th House in the Horoscope

If the lord of 8th house is placed in:

1. 1st house, the person suffers from a protracted illness, is well educated, watchful of his personal interest, earns livelihood by government service and is likely to be involved in lot of controversies.
2. 2nd house and if it is benefic planet, then it is beneficial to him; however, he becomes a victim of government wrath. If malefic, the person has a short span of life and is beset with enemies and thieves.
3. 3rd house, then the person is opposed to his brothers and friends, is harsh of speech, is devoid of a limb or part of it, is of unsteady mind and may have no brother.
4. 4th house, the person is opposed to his father. His father is sickly and he gains money from his mother.
5. 5th house and if it is benefic, he has many sons. If it is malefic planet, the person is devoid of a male issue; he has a short span of life and is a notorious cheat.
6. 6th house, the person is opposed to the government. If it is Jupiter, he may be devoid of a limb; if it is Venus, he may have an eye problem; if it is Moon he

may have a chronic illness; if it is Mars he would be hot-tempered; if it is Mercury he would be a coward; if it is Saturn, he would be greedy and has a miserable life. If Moon is aspected by benefic planets in his horoscope, then the bad effects would be mitigated.

7. 7th house, the person may have an abdominal illness; he is cruel in nature and has a cruel wife as well. If it is a malefic planet, the person is hostile to wife and dies on account of her.

8. 8th house, the person is strong, healthy, a businessman, has an outstanding personality in the family but is somewhat deceitful.

9. 9th house, he is a killer of animals, could be a hunter, is sinful, devoid of brothers, has no assistant, is ugly looking and is unpopular but is highly regarded by the enemies of the clan.

10. 10th house, the person is a low paid government employee and is indolent. If it is malefic, he has no sons and loses his mother early in life.

11. 11th house, the person is unhappy in early life but is happy in later life and enjoys a long life. If the planet is malefic, he then has a short span of life.

12. 12th house, the person is harsh in speech, is cruel and a cheat and may be devoid of a limb. His body is devoured by crows, wolf and birds after death.

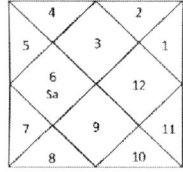

Chart shows lord of 8th house, Saturn, in 4th house in sign Virgo.

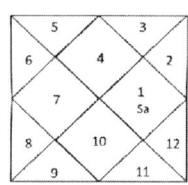

Chart shows lord of 8th house, Saturn, in 10th house in sign Aries.

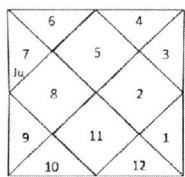

Chart shows lord of 8th house, Jupiter in 3rd house in sign Libra.

Effects of Placement of Lord of 9th House

If lord of 9th houses is placed in:

1. 1st house, the person is extremely brave; employed in government service and is devoted to gods and Brahmins but he is miserly and a sparse eater.
2. 2nd house, the person is gentle, affectionate and a great soul; he is good in the trade of bullocks but is harmed by bullocks. He may have an ugly face.
3. 3rd house, the person has a beautiful wife, may have many siblings and is very fond of brothers and sisters.
4. 4th house, the person is devoted to his father and takes care of his mother; he helps his father in his trade. He is a great soul and is very popular in the world.
5. 5th house, the person is good looking and devoted to the care of gods and Brahmins. He is a great soul and so are his sons.
6. 6th house, the person leaves tasks half completed, is impolite to his enemies and talks ill of scriptures.
7. 7th house, he has a beautiful wife who is truthful and gentle and brings good fortune to the house and the family.
8. 8th house, the person is cruel, lacking in good deeds, is killer of animals and is without a house and siblings. If the planet is malefic, the person is impotent.
9. 9th house, the person is extremely fond of his/her siblings, donates to charities, could be a guru and is god-like and is affectionate to family and spouse.
10. 10th house, the person is likely to be in government service, devoted to his/her parents, is extremely brave and famous.
11. 11th house, the person is spiritually inclined, affectionate to all, has many sons, is rich and earns his livelihood through government service.
12. 12th house, the person is handsome, well-educated and honoured in foreign countries. If it is a malefic planet, the person is a cheat.

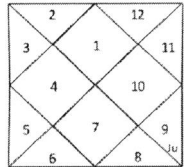
Chart shows lord of 9th house, Jupiter, in 9th house in sign Sagittarius.

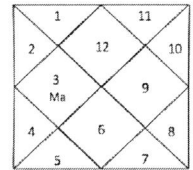
Chart shows lord of 9th house, Mars, in 4th house in sign Gemini.

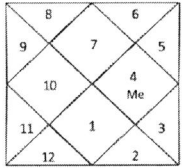
Chart shows lord of 9th house, Mercury, in 10th house in sign Cancer.

Effects of Placement of Lord of 10th House

If lord of 10th house is placed in:

1. 1st house, the person is opposed to his/her mother but is devoted to his/her father. If it is a malefic planet, then after the death of his father, his/her mother lives with another man.
2. 2nd house, the person is devoted to mother and is loved by mother; he/she is a sparse eater and lives his/her life according to the injunctions of the scriptures and *shastras*.
3. 3rd house, the person is devoted to mother, guru and his/her dependents; he/she is brave, adept in performing good deeds and triumphs over his enemies.
4. 4th house, the person has a good and noble character, is devoted to parents, is honoured by the government and lives a happy life.
5. 5th house, the person performs good actions, is gifted with music and art, gets benefited by the government. His children are looked after by his mother.
6. 6th house, the person is fearful of enemies, is cowardly, unkind, sickly and quarrelsome.
7. 7th house, the person has a beautiful wife who bears male issues, is faithful and always wishes her husband to be happy.

8. 8th house, the person is brave, cruel, devious, a cheat, has a short span of life and causes unhappiness to his/her mother.
9. 9th house, the person is gentle in nature, has good brothers and friends, his mother is devoted to performing good deeds; she is extremely kind, gentle and always speaks the truth.
10. 10th house, the person brings a lot of happiness to his mother, enjoys a number of things and happiness from his mother's family, is man of the world and adept in speaking in tune with the times.
11. 11th house, the person is rich and respected, has a long life and enjoys a lot of happiness from his mother. His mother brings him good fortune and takes good care of him.
12. 12th house, the person is given away by his mother; he is strong-willed, serves the government and performs good actions. If the planet is malefic, then he lives abroad.

Chart shows lord of 10th house in 9th house in sign Capricorn.

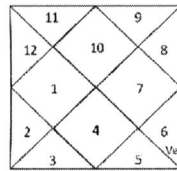

Chart shows lord of 10th house, Venus, in 9th house in sign Virgo.

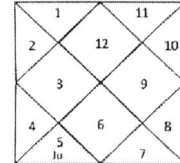

Chart shows lord of 10th house, Jupiter, in 6th house in sign Leo.

Effects of Placement of Lord of 11th House in Horoscope

If lord of 11th house is placed in:

1. 1st house, the person is strong, handsome, brave, giver of alms and is universally popular. He/she dies early in life on account of greed.
2. 2nd house and is benefic, then the person is rich. If it is malefic, the person has a short span of life and

enjoys only a few luxuries of life, is sickly and unfortunate.
3. 3rd house, the person enjoys good health, takes good care of his wife and brothers and is affectionate to them and destroys the enemies of his brothers.
4. 4th house, the person enjoys a long life, is devoted to religion and his father, is punctual in his habits and gains from all kinds of undertakings.
5. 5th house, the person loves his father and his sons, has good habits but has a short span of life.
6. 6th house, the person is hemmed in by enemies and suffers from a protracted illness. If it is a malefic planet, he dies abroad in the hands of his enemies.
7. 7th house, the person is gentle, rich, influential, authoritative, has a long life and a devoted wife.
8. 8th house and the planet is benefic, then he enjoys good health and lives a long life. If it is a malefic planet, he is sickly, unhappy and has a short span of life.
9. 9th house, the person has an expertise and knowledge of many subjects and scriptures, is devoted to gods and guru. If the planet is malefic, the person is without brothers.
10. 10th house, the person is devoted to mother, opposed to father, is rich, a scholar or pundit, has a long life and takes care of many dependents.
11. 11th house, the person has a long life, has many sons and grandsons, performs good actions, is handsome and gentle and is a leader among men, has a healthy constitution and is a good psychologist.
12. 12th house, the person enjoys whatever is available, has a stable nature, may be sickly and can occasionally create problems, is generally respected and lives a happy life.

Chart shows lord of 11th house, Venus, in 1st house in sign Sagittarius.

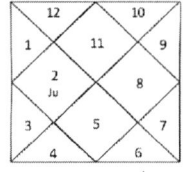
Chart shows lord of 11th house, Jupiter, in 4th house in sign Taurus.

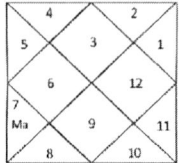
Chart shows lord of 11th house, Mars, in 5th house in sign Libra.

Effects of Placement of Lord of 12th House in the Horoscope

If the lord of 12th house is placed in the:

1. 1st house, the person is sweet of tongue, has a handsome body, lives abroad, is extravagant, remains a bachelor throughout his life.
2. 2nd house, the person is harsh of tongue, miserly, poor, could be a thief, is scared of fire and dies at a place of pilgrimage.
3. 3rd house and it is a benefic planet, then the person is rich, has a few brothers but lives away from them. If it is a malefic planet, the person is devoid of brothers.
4. 4th house, the person is sickly, miserly, performs good deeds but is usually miserable and dies on account of the actions of his sons.
5. 5th house and if it is a benefic planet, he is rich on account of his father's wealth, has sons and is usually incapable of any independent actions. If it is malefic, the person has no children.
6. 6th house and if it is a malefic planet, the person has an eye problem and dies in an unsavoury place. If the planet is Venus, the person is blind. If it is a benefic planet, these effects are mitigated.
7. 7th house, the person has a bad character and an evil person but is clever in speech. If it is a malefic planet, he dies on account of his wife; if it is a benefic planet, he dies at the hands of a prostitute.

8. 8th house and if it is a benefic planet, he hoards money. If it is a malefic planet, the person has a short span of life, is inimical to others and is incompetent in performing actions.
9. 9th house and if it is a benefic planet, the person performs many pilgrimages. If it is a malefic planet, he squanders all his money.
10. 10th house, the person has purity of heart, performs good and noble deeds. He has a strong character. His mother is harsh of tongue.
11. 11th house, the person is rich, lives a long life, owns a large house, donates to charities, speaks truth and is a famous person.
12. 12th house, the person is rich, miserly, keeps animals/pets and usually has a short span of life. If he lives long, he amasses a lot of landed property.

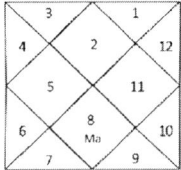

Chart shows lord of 12th house, Mars, in 7th house in sign Scorpio.

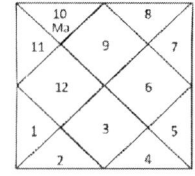

Chart shows lord of 12th house, Mars, in 2nd house in sign Capricorn.

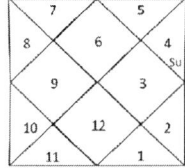

Chart shows lord of 12th house, Sun, in 11th house in sign Cancer.

Chapter V
Constellations or *Nakshtryas*

In the heavenly space, a number of groups of stars are seen arranged in various shapes and formations. Such stellar formations in the space above the earth are referred to as Constellations or *Nakshtryas*. The entire heavenly space around the earth is divided into 27 Constellations or *Nakshtryas*. These constellations are named serially as under:

I.   *Ashwani*
II.   *Bharni*
III.   *Kritka*
IV.   *Rohini*
V.   *Mrigshira*
VI.   *Ardra*
VII.   *Punarvasu*
VIII. *Pukshya*
IX.   *Aashleysha*
X.   *Magha*
XI.   *Purva-Phalguni*
XII.   *Uttar-Phalguni*
XIII. *Hasta*
XIV.   *Chitra*
XV.   *Swati*
XVI.   *Vishaka*
XVII. *Anuradha*
XVIII. *Jyeshta*
XIX.   *Moola*
XX.   *Purva-Khara*
XXI.   *Uttra-Khara*

XXII. Shravan
XXIII. Dhanishta
XXIV. Shatbhika
XXV. Purva-Bhadrapad
XXVI. Uttra-Bhadrapad
XXVII. Revti

Each constellation is split into 4 parts, called "*charans*". Thus, taken together, these 27 constellations are made up of 108 parts or *charans*. There being 12 zodiacal signs representing the space around the earth, each of these zodiacal signs corresponds to 9 *charans* of the constellations. The chart given below shows the relationship between the 12 zodiacal signs and the 27 constellations.

Zodiacal Sign	Corresponding Constellation
Aries(1)	4 charans of Ashwini (1), 4 *charans* of *Bharni* (II) and 1st charan of *Kritka* (Ill)
Taurus(2)	Last 3 charans of Kritka (Ill), 4 charans of Rohini(IV) and the first 2 charans of Mrigshira(V)
Gemini(3)	Last 2 *charans* of *Mrigshira* (IV), 4 *charans* of Ardra (VI) and the first 3 *charans* of *Punarvasu*(VII)
Cancer(4)	Last *charan* of *Punarvasu* (VII), 4 *charans* of *Pukshya* (VIII) and 4 *charans* of Aashlesha (IX)

Leo(5)	4 *charans* of *Magha* (X), 4 *charans* of *Purva-Phalguni* (XI) and the first *charan* of Uttar-*Phalguni* (XII)
Virgo(6)	Last 3 *charans* of *Uttar-Phalguni* (XII), 4 *charans* of Hasta (XIII) and the first two *charans* of Chitra (XIV)
Libra(7)	Last two *charans* of *Chitra* (XIV), 4 *charans* of Swati (XV) and the first three *charans* of *Vishaka*(XVI)
Scorpion(8)	Last *charan* of *Vishaka* (XVI), 4 *charans* of *Anuradha* (XVII) and 4 *charans* of *Jyeshta* (XVIII)
Sagittarius(9)	4 *charans* of *Moola* (XIX), 4 *charans* of *Purva-Khara* (XX) and first *charan* of *Uttar Khara*(XXI)
Capricorn(10)	Last 3 charansof Uttar-*Khara* (XXI), 4 *charans* of *Shravan* (XXII) and first two *charans* of *Dhanishta* (XXIII)
Aquarius(11)	Last two *charans* of *Dhanishta* (XXIII),4 *charans* of *Shatbhika* (XXIV) and the first three *charans* of *Purva-Bhadrapad* (XXV)
Pisces(12)	Last *charan* of *Purva-Bhadrapad* (XXV), 4 *charans* of *Uttar-Bhadrapad* (XXVI) and 4 *charans of Revti* (XXVII)

Names and Characteristics of 27 *Nakshtryas*

Each day of the year is marked by a particular *Nakshtrya* and this can be readily found out by referring to Indian almanac/*Panchang* or *Jantri*.

The characteristics of persons born during the prevalence of any one of the 27 *Nakshtryas* are being described hereunder:

1. *Ashwini*: Person would be rich, deft in all kinds of work, have a cheerful disposition, a pleasant speech and would be highly sociable and have many friends. He/she would be highly regarded by friends, relatives and the community and would acknowledge gratitude; would be broad-minded and generous. Good fortune starts after the age of 35.
2. *Bharni*: Person would be traditional, enjoy good health and longevity. He/she would be popular, keen to perform good deeds and keep the company of noble persons. He/she would be highly regarded by everyone. Good fortune starts after the age of 27.
3. *Kritka*: Person is likely to have excessive appetite and may be fond of pungent and sour food. He/she may be miserly, arrogant, and ungrateful, may have unpleasant relations with relatives and may have illicit sexual relations. Person is likely to be adept in carrying out any skilful task with dexterity. Good fortune would arise after the age of 29.
4. *Rohini*: Person respects tradition, is rich, extremely fond of friends and close relatives, is deft, mild in speech, extremely good in performing worldly obligations, is brave with a high moral character. He/she has faith in religion, is mindful of good advice, is kind-hearted, honoured by the government and is highly respectful of elders. If born during night, person may have a harsh temperament and would be fond of visiting foreign countries. Rise of good fortune occurs after the age of 30.

5. Mrigshira: Person is temperamental, fast moving, self-willed, is upset by trivialities, is fond of the company of opposite sex, is clever and ungrateful. Remains generally in a state of anger, is argumentative, quarrelsome, selfish and disrespectful of the views of others. Good fortune starts after the age of 28.
6. *Ardra*: Person is firm-minded, has humility, is wise and popular, not afraid of difficulties, has meagre wealth and is against hoarding money, is generous and noble. Rise of fate occurs after the age of 28.
7. *Punarvasu*: Person is firm-minded, is highly learned, philanthropic and is rich, highly respected by friends, peers and government. Has many friends, has good and obedient children, is helpful to everyone, is fond of things white in colour and is widely travelled. Rise of fate occurs after 28 years of age.
8. *Pukha*: Person is polite, good-mannered, is clever, inclined to help others, having faith in God, devoted to religious works, is of noble nature, can discriminate between good and bad. Rise of fate occurs after the age of 30 years.
9. *Ashlesha*: Person feels happy in performing noble acts, has a large family or clan, is fond of good things of life, is fond of gods, elders, sadhus and saints, is not easily exploited by others, feels happy in seeing the welfare and progress of other persons, is inclined to have addictions, not able to discriminate between good and evil, does not enjoy good relations with relatives. Rise of fate occurs after 30 years of age.
10. *Magha*: Person is principled, faithful and devoted to spouse, respectful and devoted to parents, is disinclined to trouble other persons, is rich, prosperous and highly successful in business. Fate shines after the age of 25.
11. *Purva-Phalguni*: Person overcomes his enemies, is clever in all kinds of activities, has good connections with the rich, with the officers and functionaries of

government, is of cheerful disposition, has pleasant speech, is popular and loved by the opposite sex, lives a luxurious life, has several vehicles, is highly able, competent, successful in his/her ambitions, is popular among the relatives and is highly respected by the society and the government. Fates shines after the age of 28.

12. *Uttar-Phalguni*: Person is rich, given to luxuries of life, has knowledge of armaments, is strong and brave, fond of sports and wrestling, is well mannered, well-spoken and sober in habits and is very good at talking. Rise of fate occurs after 28 years of life.

13. *Hast*: Person is leader of his clan and community, is brave and commanding, always eager to take up cudgels with enemies, is fond of intoxicating substances, lives away from brothers and relatives, is fond of luxuries, may have illicit sexual relations and may be given to anger. Good fortune may arise after the age of 30.

14. *Chitra*: Person is a great philanthropist, is rich and prosperous, has devoted spouse and children, is of cheerful temperament, is fond of construction activities, knows Vedas and has noble and spiritual thoughts and may not be able to store much money. Good fortune develops between 33 and 38 years of age.

15. *Swati*: Person is wise and well versed in business activities, looks after his relatives and friends, is of cool temperament, is popular and highly social and is devoted to gods. Good fortune may arise between 30 and 34 years of life.

16. *Vishaka*: Person is handsome, fortunate and rich, may occasionally be inclined towards controversial activities, is opportunistic, is firm-minded and commands respect, enjoys polemics and quarrels, is brave and courageous, has pleasant manners and pleasant speech and is widely travelled. Rise of good fortune occurs between 21 and 28 years of life.

17. *Anuradha*: Person is learned, talented, is expert in business and all kinds of trades, arts and skills, is much respected, is prosperous, polite and humble, has a big appetite, and looks after family and clan and travels a lot. Good fortune rises after 39 years of age.
18. *Jyeshta*: Person is very rich, is highly religious, is noble and philanthropic, is fond of trade and industry, is sophisticated and fond of poetry, is polite and even-tempered, and is dutiful and clever. Rise of good fortune occurs after 30 years of age.
19. *Moola*: Person is learned, happy, serious-minded, is popular and highly respected by his community, is prone to illnesses and is upset by trivialities. Rise of good fortune occurs between 27 and 31 years of age.
20. *Purva-kharda*: Person is good in negotiations and in uniting people, is highly intelligent, is friendly to all and helpful to everyone, especially helpful to the poor and afflicted persons and is clever. Rise of good fortune occurs at 28 years of life.
21. *Uttar-kharda*: Person is fond of the company of rich persons, is very intelligent and highly knowledgeable, is successful in all activities of life, has many friends and is well-wisher of everyone, is highly popular and respected by all and is very fond of music. Rise of fortune occurs in 31st year of life.
22 *Shravan*: Person is rich, well-spoken, and brave, has good reputation, has a beautiful wife, is fond of music, accounts and astrology, has a broad vision of life and is able to read the mind of others. Good fortune rises after 25 years of age.
23. *Ghanishta*: Person has a noble nature, is fond of music, is devoted to wife, kith and kin, is courageous and devoted to virtuous deeds, works for the government, is popular in public and government circles and possesses many jewels and precious stones. Good fortune rises after 30 years of age.
24. *Shat-bhaka*: Person is rich, known for his good manners and sophistication, is devoted to noble

deeds, is generous and sympathetic, may have illicit relations, dominates enemies, and is highly respected everywhere. Good fortune occurs at 28 years of age.

25. *Purva-bhadurpad*: Person is rich, cheerful and highly talkative, loves near and dear ones, is highly talented, is fond of sleep and comforts and enjoys the obedience of his children. Fortune rises at 19 years of age.

26. *Uttar-bhadurpad*: Person is very famous, very fair and handsome, very brave and influential, is a great orator and a skilful talker, skilful in arguments, is generous and opportunistic, overcomes all enemies, has knowledge of religion and knows art of diplomacy, is firm-footed and dutiful. Good fortune rises at 27 or 31 years of age.

27. Revti: Person is devoted to his/her parents, is fast moving, talks fast, generous and well-wisher of everyone and happy in the company of friends. Rise of good fortune occurs after 25 years of age.

Table showing the Nakshtryas, their Zodiacal signs and their Lordship:

Zodiacal Sign	Corresponding Constellation	Ruling Planet
Aries (1)	4 charans of *Ashwani* (I), 4 charans of *Bharni* (II) and 1st charan of *Kritka* (III)	Mars
Taurus (2)	Last 3 charans of *Kritka* (III), 4 charans of *Rohni* (IV) and first two charans of *Mrigshira* (V)	Venus
Gemini (3)	Last 2 charans of *Mrigshira* (V), 4 charans of *Ardra* (VI) and first 3 charans of *Punarvasu* (VII)	Mercury
Cancer (4)	Last charan of *Punarvasu* (VII), 4 charans of *Pukshya* (VIII) and 4 charans of *Aashleysha* (IX)	Moon
Leo (5)	4 charans of *Magha* (X), 4 charans of *Purva-Phalguni* (XI) and first charan of *Uttarphalguni* (XII)	Sun
Virgo (6)	Last 3 charans of *Uttar-Phalguni* (XII), 4 charans of *Hasta* (XIII) and first two charans of *Chitra* (XIV)	Mercury

Libra (7)	Last two *charans* of *Chitra* (XIV), 4 *charans* of *Swati* (XV) and first three *charans* of *Vishaka* (XVI)	Venus
Scorpio (8)	Last *charan* of *Vishaka* (XVI), 4 *charans* of *Anuradha* (XVII) and 4 *charans* of *Jyeshta* (XVIII)	Mars
Sagittarius (9)	4 *charans* of *Moola* (XIX), 4 *charans* of *Purva-Khara* (XX) and first *charan* of *Uttar-Khada* (XXI)	Jupiter
Capricorn (10)	Last 3 *charans* of *Uttar-Khara* (XXI), 4 *charans* of *Shravan* (XXII) and first two *charans* of *Dhanishta* (XXIII)	Saturn
Aquarius	Last 2 *charans* of *Dhanishta* (XXIII), 4 *charans* of *Shatbhika* (XXIV) and first 3 charans of *Purva-Bhadrapad* (XXV)	Saturn
Pisces (12)	Last *charan* of *Purva-Bhadrapad* (XXV), 4 *charans* of *Uttar-Bhadrapad* (XXVI) and 4 *charans* of *Revti* (XXVII)	Jupiter

Importance of *Nakshtryas*

Nakshtryas play a significant role in three areas of vital importance in the life of a person. These are:

1. *Muhurat* or Auspicious Time: Indian astrology believes that there is a favourable time in starting an important activity/a new enterprise in life and that choosing an auspicious or favourable time is likely to lead to a successful outcome in the activity. This is known as *Muhurat*. Examples of such occasions include deciding on time and date of joining a school, time and date of a wedding, time and date of starting a new hob, time and date of starting a new business or enterprise, time and date of filing nomination papers for elections or time and date of filing a lawsuit in court etc.
2. Matching Horoscopes for Matrimony: *Nakshtrya* of the prospective groom and bride are matched in the Indian system of astrology to determine whether they would have a happy, harmonious and convivial married life or otherwise. The matching is done by using a chart which indicates the points scored in the matching process.
3. What sort of day would I have today?
   Again the answer to this question is largely governed by the prevailing *Nakshtrya* of that day and the relationship between this and the birth *Nakshtrya* of the person.

These areas would be taken up in detail and discussed in the Section on Prediction and *Phaladesh*.

Chapter VI
Yogas

Yoga means union. Union, conjunctions, combinations and permutations of planets in a particular house/houses and the relationship of such combinations/permutations with other planets and houses in a horoscope constitute what is termed as a Yoga. There may be one or several Yogas in a horoscope chart. The Yogas have significant and "uncanny" effects on the life and fortune of a person, usually quite independent of other factors or considerations in a horoscope.

There are a large number of Yogas described in Indian astrology.

Some of these Yogas are known as "Raj Yogas". Raja means a king. There are very few kings left now in modern times. In Indian astrology, a Raj Yoga or kingly Yoga means a very high or topmost position in business, government, social, political, administrative or any other sphere of activity of a person.

Some of the Important Yogas and Their Effects

1. *Sinhasan* Yoga (Kingship Yoga): If all the planets in a horoscope are in the 2nd, 3rd, 6th, 8th and 12th houses, such a person ascends to the throne as king.
2. *Hans* Yoga (*Hamsa*): If all the planets in a horoscope chart are placed in 1st, 5th, 7th and 9th house, the person supports and provides livelihood to his/her entire family and clan.

3. *Dwaj* Yoga: If malefic planets are in the 8th house and the benefic planets are in the 1st house, such a person is a great social leader.
4. *Karika* Yoga: If all the planets are in the 10th and 11th house or alternatively in the 1st and 7th house, such a person, even if born in a poor family, becomes a king.
5. *Chatusar* Yoga: If all the planets are in the 4 *kendras*, i.e. in the 1st, 4th, 7th and 10th house, such a person is a wealthy ruler and all his enemies are destroyed.
6. *Ekavali* Yoga: If the seven planets, excluding Rahu and Ketu, are placed consecutively in 7 houses in a sequence starting from the 1st house or any other house, such a person becomes a ruler even if born in a poor family.
7. Amar Yoga: If all the malefic planets are in the 4 *kendras*, the person is a cruel ruler. Alternatively, if all the benefic planets are placed in 4 *kendras*, such a person would be a benign ruler.
8. *Vapi* Yoga: If all the planets are placed in houses other than 1st, 2nd and 12th house, such a person becomes outstanding in his clan, has a long life, is virtuous, sweet of tongue, outstandingly brave commander, wealthy, of steady mind and is happy.
9. Yup Yoga: If the seven planets, excluding Rahu and Ketu, are placed in the 1st house, 2nd house, 3rd house and 4th house, such a person is of steady mind, generous, performer of *Yajnas* (sacrificial rituals), is highly learned, wealthy and outstanding among men.
10. *Shur* Yoga: If the 7 planets are in the 4th, 5th, 6th and 7th houses, such a person is expert in archery, is lover of forest life, unable to enjoy even a beautiful wife, woe-ridden and is very aggressive and violent.
11. Shakti Yoga: If the 7 planets are in the 7th house, 8th house, 9th house and 10th house, such a person is adept in warfare, is indolent, bereft of happiness, argumentative, affectionate to the young and the elderly and enjoys very little of domestic happiness.

12. *Dand* Yoga: If all the 7 planets are placed in the 10th house, 11th house, 12th house and 1st house, such person would be poor, of lowly deeds, enjoys happiness from highly placed persons, is bereft of wife, children, wealth and education and is inimical to his own family.
13. *Chakra* Yoga: Starting from the 1st house, if the 7 planets are placed in alternate houses, i.e., in the 1st house, 3rd house, 5th house, 7th house, 9th house and 11th house, such a person would be handsome, highly respected, highly successful commander, is honoured by the government, is highly influential and has international renown.
14. *Samudra* Yoga: Starting from the 2nd house, if all the 7 planets are placed in alternate houses, i.e. in the 2nd, 4th, 6th, 8th, 10th and 12th house, such a person is charitable, of steady mind, is respected and influential, famous and enhances the reputation of his family.
15. *Gole* Yoga: If all the 7 planets are placed in a single house, such a person is bereft of education, strength, intelligence and resourcefulness; he is undiplomatic, liar and is poor.
16. *Yug* Yoga: If the 7 planets are placed in only two houses in a horoscope, such a person is shameless, is devoid of wealth and sons, lacks faith in religion and ability to discriminate between right and wrong.
17. *Shool* Yoga: If the 7 planets, other than Rahu and Ketu, are located in three houses in a horoscope, such a person is untrustworthy, engaged in condemnable activities, is cruel, is a cheat, poor, adept in getting into controversy, and is a prickly character and a thorn in the flesh of others.
18. *Kedar* Yoga: If 7 planets are located in four houses, such a person is truthful, wealthy, victorious, obliging, of steady mind, of good character, is adept in farming and is grateful for help from others.

19. *Pash* Yoga: If the 7 planets are placed in five houses in a horoscope, such a person is poor in constitution, is jealous and mean, not wishing well of others, is unhappy, makes false promises with ready explanations, a useless talker, draws wrong and contrary inferences from facts and figures and is fond of forest and outdoor life.
20. *Damini* Yoga: If the 7 planets are placed in 6 houses in a horoscope, such a person is of steady mind, learned, charitable, famous, has many offspring, always happy, gentle and of good character but can get angry.
21. *Veena* Yoga: If the 7 planets are placed in seven houses in a horoscope, such a person is rich, has knowledge of scriptures, adept in doing all kinds of things, provides livelihood to a large number of persons and enjoys all the good things of life.
22. *Shakat* Yoga: If the 7 planets are placed in the 1st and 7th house, such a person makes his livelihood by working as a driver.
23. Nanda Yoga: If the 7 planets are placed two each in 3 houses or alternatively if three planets each are placed in two houses, it is Nanda Yoga. Such a person is happy and lives a long life and is honoured and respected by the ruler.
24. *Sarvarthdari* Yoga: If Jupiter is in 1st house, Venus is in 4th house, Mercury is in 7th house and Mars is in 10th house, such a person has fulfilment of his/her desires.
25. *Rajhans* Yoga: If all the planets are in the signs of Aries, Leo, Libra and Aquarius, such a person is like a raja or king and enjoys happiness in life.
26. *Safaldola* Yoga: If the feminine planets, i.e. Venus and Moon are in Aries, Sagittarius or Pisces, such a person attains to kingdom.
27. *Rajmantritva* Yoga: If Jupiter is free of any malefic planet and is in any of the Kendras, such a person is charitable, highly reputed, virtuous, artistic, a

musician, dancer, rich, happy, diplomatic and is a Minister to the ruler.

28. *Swesha-Mrittu* Yoga: If Mars is in any of the 4 Kendras and Rahu is in 7th house, such a person dies according to his/her own wish.

29. *Unfa* Yoga: If any planet is placed in the 12th house from the position of Moon that is *Unfa* Yoga. Effects are: (a) if it is Mars, the person is a leader of thieves, reputed, proud, independent, hot-tempered, quarrelsome, and adept in warfare, of good health and handsome body, shameless and adds to his wealth. (b) If it is Mercury, the person is a musician, good in writing, could be a poet, a preacher, radiant and handsome, honoured by king, famous and engaged in a highly reputed profession. (c) If it is Jupiter, such a person is an intellectual, wise, could be an outstanding poet, honoured by the ruler and is famous. (d) If it is Venus, such a person is very popular, wise, handsome, rich, full of gold, liked by the ruler and is clever. (e) If it is Saturn, the person is well-built, handsome, keeper of many animals, true to the word of his mouth, is long-limbed, virtuous, has many sons and cohabitates with ladies of low repute.

30. *Sunfa* Yoga: If any planet other than the Sun is in the 2nd house to the placement of Moon, it is called *Sunfa* Yoga. (a) If it is Mars, then the person earns his/her livelihood by hard work, is harsh of tongue, is aggressive, opposed to many persons and is a brave person.

(b) If it is Mercury, the person is highly religious, a poet, musician, knower of scriptures, well-wisher of everyone and has handsome personality (c) If it is Jupiter, the person is learned in many spheres, is loved by the king and possesses many material things of life.

(d) If it is Venus, the person has a lot of farming land and animals, is influential, has a beautiful spouse, is brave and adept in doing many things and is honoured by the king (e) If it is Saturn, person has highly developed sense of discrimination, is extremely wealthy, is famous, keeps his/her activities secret, is honoured by the residents of the town of his/her residence but has a bad heart.

31. *Durdhara* Yoga: Placement of planets other than the Sun in the 2nd house, as well as the 12th house from the placement of Moon constitutes *Durdhara* Yoga. (a) If Mars and Mercury make this Yoga, the person is a liar, a cheat, greedy, outstanding in the family and clan, highly competent in work, has many qualities and is very rich (b) If Mars and Venus constitute this Yoga, the person is very handsome, courageous, brave, loves physical exercise, adept in warfare and brave in war, is argumentative and has a gentle and devoted spouse (c) If Mars and Jupiter constitute this Yoga, then the person is devious, shameless, thrifty, is opposed to many people, but is famous for his good actions (d) If Mars and Saturn constitute this Yoga, the person is expert in sexual activities, given to overindulgence in sex, hot-tempered, carries tales, has many enemies and gathers a lot of money (e) If Mercury and Jupiter constitute this Yoga, the person is a knower of scriptures, has knowledge of religion, is a good orator, gives alms, increases his wealth and is famous in the world (f) If Mercury and Venus constitute this Yoga, the person is a good soul, happy, brave, could be a Minister in the government, has a radiant personality, is sweet of tongue and is extremely busy in worldly activities and is famous. (g) If Mercury and Saturn constitute this Yoga, then the person travels to a large number of countries, does not attach too much importance to money, is learned, criticised and disrespected by his own people but is honoured by others.(h) If Jupiter and Venus constitute thus Yoga, then the person is well-versed in diplomacy, is of high intellect, of steady mind, serious-minded, firm, full of gold and precious

stones, known for something to everyone, honoured by the government and is a government servant (i) If Jupiter and Saturn constitute this Yoga, then the person is expert in diplomacy, could be a scientist, is happy, sweet of tongue, has many issues, is learned and highly competent in doing all kinds of things (j) If Venus and Saturn constitute this Yoga then the person has a knowledge of large number of fields, is honoured by the ruler, is adept in doing all kinds of things, has a very good family background, is popular among the ladies and has a wife older than himself.

32. *Kemdrum* Yoga: Absence of any planet in the 12th and 2nd house from the position of Moon constitutes *Kemdrum* Yoga. Person born with this Yoga is bereft of spouse and children, is unhappy, is an aimless talker, wears unclean clothes, has a low mind, is a coward, harbours condemnable thoughts, is of poor character and has a long life. If Moon is in a Kendra or is in conjunction with another planet, then *Kemdrum* Yoga is cancelled and the person wins victory over others and attains the rulership of a large kingdom.

33. *Voshi* Yoga: Excepting Moon, if any other planet is placed 12th to the position of Sun then this constitutes *Voshi* Yoga (a) If Jupiter is such a planet, then the person gathers and saves a lot of money and is famous (b) If it is Venus, then the person is cowardly, sex indulgent, indolent and dependent on others (c) If it is Mercury, then the person has delicate manners, is polite but is shameless, is poor and is subject to the criticism of others, (d) If it is Mars, then the person looks after the interest of others but is against his mother, (e) If it is Saturn, then the person is controversial, has the constitution of an old person and has illicit relations with another woman.

34. *Veshi* Yoga: If any of the five planets other than Moon is in the 2nd house to position of Sun, this is said to be *Veshi* Yoga. (a) If it is Jupiter, then the

person is of steady mind, speaks truth, is intelligent and is brave in war(b) If it is Venus, then the person is famous in the world, is full of virtues and is a great person (c) If it is Mercury, the person is sweet in speech, is handsome but is harmful to others(d) If it is Mars, then the person is an excellent driver and earns fame at the war front(e) If it is Saturn, the person is expert in commercial matters, snatches other persons' money and is opposed to gurus.

35. *Ubhaychari* Yoga: If planets other than Moon happen to be placed in the 2nd house and the 12th house to the position of Sun in a horoscope, it constitutes *Ubhaychari* Yoga. Such a person has the capacity to tolerate hardships with equipoise or balanced mind, is of medium height, has a steady and firm mind, is serious-minded, is "*satoguni*", adept in doing all kinds of things, has a strong neck, is handsome, has many domestic servants, gives shelter to brothers, is physically fit and strong, enjoys all the good things of life, is wealthy, happy and full of valour and courage like a king.

36. *Mahasagar* Yoga: If Mercury, Jupiter, Venus and Moon are placed in the 1st house, 4th house, 7th house and 10th house respectively and Mars is in the 6th house and Rahu is in the 3rd house, then this is called *Mahasagar* Yoga. Such a person is either a ruler or a Minister in the government, is devoted to Brahmins and gods and has some illness due to a war injury.

37. *Daaridrya* Yoga: (a) If malefic planets are placed in all the four Kendras, then the person is poor (b) If all the malefic planets are placed in the 2nd house, then the person is poor.

38. *Shakra* Yoga: If Sun in Aries sign is placed in the 11th house, Jupiter in sign Cancer is placed in 2nd house and Venus in Pisces is placed in 10th house, then the person is said to have *Shakra* Yoga. Such a person worships Brahmins and gods, has an exceptional

power of memory, has a radiant personality, is renowned, a great soul, full of courage and valour and is famous. He is unable to hoard money and is beset with anxieties. He serves sadhus, is famous among people and performs great deeds and earns fame like a king.

39. *Darun* Yoga: If Sun is in 6th or 8th house, other malefic planets are in 6th or 8th house and benefic planets are placed in *Kendras* or in *Trikon*, then the person has *Darun* Yoga. Such a person is a knower of scriptures, is rich, religious-minded, having many domestic servants, is virtuous and speaks in many social meetings. He faces a lot of hardship up to the age of 16 years of age and again faces some hardship at the age of 36.

40. *Veepak* Yoga: When all the *Kendras* are empty and all the malefic planets are placed in the 5th, 8th and 9th house, it is said to be Veal Yoga. Such a person is brave like a king but has an evil mind. He enjoys many sons and brothers but is troubled and persecuted by his enemies and by the ruler later in life. He has anxiety due to lack of money.

41. *Chakradamni* Yoga: If Jupiter is placed in the sign of Mercury, Venus is placed in the sign of Jupiter and Moon is placed in the house of Venus, then it is *Chakradamni* Yoga. Such a person has large lotus-like eyes, has a long life, is brave, clever, competent in doing all kind of things, is intelligent, has landed property and is not very fond of sex.

42. *Rajmanya* Yoga: This includes a number of Raj *Yogas*. These denote a high status like that of a king or the ruler.

    Some of these are described here: (a) If Moon is in 1st house in sign Taurus and the other 6 planets are exalted in any of the other houses, the person is powerful and brave like a king (b) If all the planets are in *Mooi-Trikon* or alternatively placed in conjunction with Mars in any house in a friendly sign and are not debilitated in *Navamsh* (c) If Moon and Jupiter are placed in the 1st house, Venus is in 10th house and Saturn is in Libra, Capricorn or Aquarius (d) If all the benefic planets are placed in the 1st house, 2nd house, 3rd house, 10th house and 11th house (e) If benefic planets are placed in *Kendras* or *Trikons* and the malefic planets are placed in 3rd, 6th and 11th houses (f) If there is conjunction of Mercury and Jupiter in any house or Mercury aspecting Jupiter or the Jupiter is in Sagittarius or Pisces (g) Moon is in Kendra and is aspected by Jupiter and Venus is strong (h) A debilitated planet in *Janam Kundli* gets exalted in *Navansh* (i) Jupiter is in 1st house, Mercury is in a Kendra and is aspected by the lord of the 9th house (j) Jupiter in 5th, 7th or 9th house is aspected by the lord of the 1st house (k) Saturn is in a Kendra, 5th or 9th house or is exalted or in its *Mooi-Trikon* and is aspecting the 10th house (I) *Debilitated* Jupiter is in 1st house and Lord of 9th house is in the 8th *Navamsh* of Moon (m) All planets are placed consecutively from 1st house to 6th house (n) Lord of 9th house is placed along with Moon in the 2nd house (o) Malefic planets plus the Lord of 10th house are placed consecutively from 1st house to 6th house (p) Lord of the sign in which Moon is placed in *Navamsh*, gets placed in Kendra, in *Trikon* or in 11th house or is placed in conjunction with Mercury (q) Moon is in conjunction with Mars in the 2nd or 3rd house or Moon is in conjunction with Rahu in the 5th house (r) Lord of 9th house in *Navamsh* is in conjunction with Rahu in 4th house (s) Conjunction of Saturn and Rahu in Pisces is aspected by the lord of 9th house or alternatively the lord of 1st house is debilitated (t) Moon in Pisces sign is in 1st house, Sun is in Leo, Mars is in Capricorn and Saturn is in Aquarius (u) Mars in sign Aries is placed in 1st house (v) Jupiter in sign Aries is in 1st house, Moon is in 4th house and Venus is in 10th house (w) Sun and Venus are in 2nd house, Moon and Jupiter are in Kendra and are not eclipsed or aspected by any malefic planets (x) Jupiter and Venus are in the 4th house (y) If any planet is placed in its 5th *Navamsh* (z) If Jupiter is aspected by Mercury, the person is extremely rich (al) Moon is in the *Navamsh* of Venus and is aspected by Venus (bl) Moon is in its own *Navamsh* and is aspected by Jupiter(cl) Sun and Moon are in Aries (dl) If all the planets are in 7th, 12th, 1st and 2nd house (el) If Venus, Jupiter and Mercury are in 2nd house and Mars and Moon are in 7th house, the person scores victory over his enemies and is a powerful king (fl) All planets are placed in 3rd, 6th,10th and 11th house (gl) Mercury is in Cancer, Jupiter is in Sagittarius, Mercury is aspected by Sun and Jupiter is aspected by Mars (hl) Rahu and Mars are in 6th house and Sun and Mercury are in 10th house (il) If all the planets are placed between Jupiter and Saturn (jl) Jupiter is in 3rd house and Saturn is in 8th house and the rest of the planets are placed between them(kl) Jupiter is in 3rd house and Moon is in 11th house (11) Jupiter is in 5th house and Moon is in 10th house (ml) Jupiter is in Leo and the other planets are in signs Cancer, Libra, Sagittarius and Capricorn (nl) Jupiter is in Leo, Venus is in Virgo, Saturn is in Gemini and Mars is in its own sign in 4th house (ol) Malefic planets are in 8th and 12th houses and the other planets are placed between these two (pl) Saturn and Moon are in Sagittarius, Jupiter is in Aries and Venus and Rahu are in 10thhouse (ql) All planets are in 6th, 8th, 12th and 2nd house (rl) Exalted malefic planets in 1st house make a Raja who is poor (sl) *Gaj-Kesri* yoga: Conjunction of Moon and Jupiter, Moon and Jupiter aspecting each other or Jupiter aspecting Moon constitute this yoga. It is an important Raj Yoga and confers numerous beneficial effects on the individual.

Comments:

Raja means a king. There are not many kings or any *Rajas* in existence any more in modern times. The above *Raj* Yogas mean that the person would have a very high status or position in life and in the world something like a president, prime minister, governor, chief minister, minister, ambassador, CEO, chairman, chief of army staff, commander, director, chairman, chief justice, administrator etc.

Chapter VII
Prediction or *Phaladesh**
Art and Science of Prediction

This is the most important chapter of the book. Prediction or forecasting the future or *Phaladesh* is based primarily on the house of placement and the sign of each of the nine planets in the horoscope chart of an individual. Overall, skill in predicting the future on the basis of astrological data of a person, is an art, part-science and part-intuition.

This is being considered under several headings. These are:

A. Familiarity with Indian almanac or *Panchang* or *Jantri*.
B. General Guidelines.
C. Different Horoscope Charts.
D. Concept of Benefic and Malefic Planets.
E. General assessment of the twelve houses of a horoscope.
F. Detailed systematic assessment of the twelve houses of a horoscope.
G. *Dasha* or the Reigning Period of Planets in the Life of an Individual.
H. Miscellaneous Issues:
a) Answering questions
b) Matching horoscopes
c) My today

---

*Phaladesh is the Sanskrit equivalent of prediction.

I. Some Illustrating Horoscopes

Familiarity with Indian Almanac, *Panchang* or *Jantri*

Indian almanac is known colloquially as *Panchang* or *Jantri*. This is readily available in the market in Hindi, Urdu or any of the regional languages of India.

The *Jantri* is an indispensable and an essential tool for every student and practitioner of Indian astrology. It provides ready, factual, mathematically worked out, essential vital data required in the interpretation of horoscopes for prediction.

It is a kind of a calendar containing 12 pages for each of the 12 months of the year besides other astrological data.

Each month consists of a lunar and solar fortnight which are called "*Krishan Paksha*" (dark fortnight) and "*Shukla Paksha*" (bright fortnight) respectively. These correspond to the waning and waxing fortnights of Moon. There are 15 days in the dark fortnight and 15 days in the bright fortnight. Each day is called a "*tithe*" in Sanskrit. There are, therefore "15 *tithes*" in dark fortnight and 15 "tithes" in bright fortnight.

There are several columns on each page of the almanac. These columns depict the time of sunrise and sunset, the "*tithi*", in a chronological order in the lunar/solar fortnight, the "*Nakshtrya*" of the day, Moon sign of the day and the placement of 9 planets in different signs on that day. In addition, a lot of other relevant information is contained in the *Panchang* e.g. "*lagan sarni*" to help find the ascendant/lagan of a new born, matching the horoscopes of prospective bride and groom, auspicious dates for marriage, starting a new business or a new job, auspicious dates for undertaking a journey, pilgrimage etc.

Placement of nine planets in the twelve houses of a horoscope chart and the assignment of a particular zodiacal sign in each of those houses, forms the basis of making predictions or *phaladesh*.

General Guidelines:

1. There is no difference in *phaladesh* or prediction whether the horoscope belongs to a male or a female.
2. Joint Family: Destinies of people living with other members of the family in a joint family are linked to each other to some extent. Individual horoscope of each person affects the others to some extent. Horoscope of a person is affected to some extent by the horoscope of the spouse. Horoscopes of dependent children affect the horoscopes of their parents and siblings. Horoscope of the bread winner is considerably affected by the horoscopes of all dependent children whereas the horoscopes of children are affected to a lesser degree by the horoscope of the bread winner. The horoscope of a close friend also affects the horoscope of a person to some extent.
3. *Kendras*: 1st, 4th, 7th and 10th houses in a horoscope chart are called *Kendras*. *Kendra* means a centre. Planets placed in *Kendras* are more powerful than when they are placed in other houses of the horoscope chart.
4. Planets located in *Trikons*, i.e., 5th and 9th houses, exercise a powerful influence on the life of a person.
5. Planets placed in the 2nd and 11th house exercise a very important positive influence on the wealth and material gains in the life of a person especially the 11th house.
6. Planets placed in the 3rd house enhance the courage, will power and determination of a person in a positive manner by virtue of which he/she goes from strength to strength.
7. Planets in the 6th, 8th and 12th houses create problems and anxieties for a person because 6th house is the house of enemies, 8th house is the house of obstacles and death and 12th house is the house of losses, worries and expenses.

8. Malefic planets in 3rd, 6th and 11th house give tremendous strength to a person.
9. Every planet in the 11th house acts as benefic.
10. Planets in an exalted sign, in their own sign, in a friendly sign and planets which aspect the house of its exaltation, all add up the qualities and strength of that house. For example, Sun in Leo or Aries or aspecting these two signs, gives strength to the house aspected by it.
11. Any planet in conjunction with Sun is said to be "combust" ("*ast*" or ineffective). If such a planet is more than 6 degrees away from the Sun, it is said to be "half-combust" and if it is more than 15 degrees away from the Sun, it is said to be "non-combust", i.e., it is fully effective.
12. A malefic planet placed in 3rd house becomes benefic and gives beneficial effects in respect of the house of which it is the lord.
13. Generally, a benefic placed in a house produces good effects and a malefic planet produces adverse effects.
14. If the lord of a house is placed in that house or if any one of Venus, Mercury or Jupiter is located in that house or aspects that house or if that house is free of any planet and is not aspected by any other planet, then that house gives beneficial results to that person.
15. If the lord of a house is in conjunction with a benefic planet or is aspected by a benefic planet then that house gives beneficial results to that person.
16. If a malefic planet is placed in a house or the lord of that house is in conjunction with a malefic planet or is aspected by a malefic planet, then the effect of that house is adverse or harmful for that person.
17. If the lord of a house is exalted or is in its own sign or is in its *Mooi-Trikon*, then the effect of that house is excellent.
18. Sun, Mars, Saturn and Rahu are malefic planets in an ascending order, i.e. Mars is more malefic than Sun, Saturn is more malefic than Mars and Rahu is more

malefic than Saturn. Even when placed in their own signs, these planets have an element of harmful effect. However, when they are placed in a friendly sign or in the sign of a benefic planet or in their exalted sign, they have an overall good effect and the harmful effect is mitigated.

19. Moon, Mercury, Venus, Ketu and Jupiter are "benefic" planets in an ascending order. Thus Mercury is more benefic than Moon, Venus is more benefic than Mercury, Ketu is more benefic than Venus and Jupiter is more benefic than Ketu. Ketu is regarded "malefic" planet by some astrologers while making predictions; others consider it to be "benefic". These planets in their own signs are highly beneficial and less beneficial when located in the sign of Sun, Mars, Saturn and Rahu.

20. Planets located in 8th and 12th houses are harmful to a person to a lesser or greater degree.

21. Jupiter in the 6th house destroys enemies. Saturn in 8th house gives longevity. Mars in 10th house confers extremely good fortune.

22. Lord of 8th house wherever it happens to get placed, harms the house of its placement.

23. Rahu and Ketu harm the house where they get placed. Whichever house is harmed by Rahu is benefited by Ketu and whichever house is harmed by Ketu is benefited by Rahu.

24. If Jupiter gets located alone in the 2nd or 7th house, then its effects are contrary to the expected, for some strange reason, i.e. it harms the house in one way or another.

25. If Jupiter is located in 1st, 4th, 5th, 9th and 10th house, then it removes all the "ill-effects or afflictions" (*doshas*) from that horoscope, i.e. it removes one hundred to a thousand afflictions or *doshas*.

26. If Sun is located in 11th house or Moon is in good sign in the 1st house, they destroy nine ill-effects or afflictions from that horoscope.
27. Mercury in 1st, 4th, 5th, 9th or 10th house removes 100 ill-effects or afflictions from that horoscope.
28. Venus in any of the five houses, 1st, 4th, 5th, 9th and 10th, removes 200 afflictions or *doshas* from that horoscope.
29. Lord of ascendant (lagan) in 4th, 10th or 11th house removes many afflictions or *doshas* from that horoscope.

(Italicised words are Sanskrit equivalents)

Different Horoscope Charts

In Chapter II on page 18, it was mentioned that the professional astrologer usually prepares several horoscope charts while casting/preparing the horoscope or *Janam Patri* of a newborn or a grown-up person. These charts are named as: 1. *Janam Kundli* or *Janamangam* or basic birth chart. 2. *Chander Kundli* with Moon in the ascendant. 3. *Surya Kundli* having Sun in the ascendant. 4. *Hora Chakra* indicating mainly the wealth of a person. 5. *Saptansh Kundli* which is mainly taken into account when predicting about the children of a person. 6. *Navamsh* chart: This is a very important chart in astrology and is taken into account when predicting about any sphere of activity in the life of a person particularly his/her married life, the spouse and the profession of the person. 7. *Dreshkan*. 8. *Dwadshamsh* and 9. *Trishamsh*. The last three charts are also considered in the overall assessment of the life of a person and 10. *Gochar* chart: this chart shows the current position of planets in the horoscope of a person. It is prepared by having an empty chart with 12 houses, keeping the ascendant sign as the 1st house in the chart. The current position of planets is then noted down from the *Panchang* and is inserted in the 12 houses and this is known as *Gochar* chart or horoscope. This chart is of particular importance when one is required to answer any question from the client and is also sometimes referred to as *"Prashna Kundli"*. *Gochar* chart is also of great value in finding out what sort of a day a person is going to have.

For practical purposes, the reader would profit by making use of *Janam Kundli*, *Chander Kundli*, *Surya Kundli*, *Navamsh Kundli* and *Gochar Kundli* when making predictions or for *Phaladesh*.

Concept of Benefic and Malefic Planets

Moon, Mercury, Venus, Ketu and Jupiter are benefic planets in an ascending order. Thus Mercury is more benefic than Moon; Venus is more benefic than Mercury; Ketu is more benefic than Venus and Jupiter is more benefic than Ketu.

Ketu is considered as malefic by some astrologers while others consider it as benefic. The consensus is that when Ketu is in conjunction with any of the benefic planets, it is benefic and when it is in conjunction with malefic planets, it has malefic propensity.

Generally, the benefic planets produce beneficial effects and the malefic planets give harmful effects.

Malefic planets in 3rd, 6th, and 11th house have benefic effects.

Every planet in 11th house acts as benefic.

Even when placed in their own sign, the malefic planets have an element of causing some harm. However, when placed in a friendly sign or in the sign of a benefic planet or in their exalted sign, they have an overall benefic effect and the harmful effect is mitigated.

General Assessment of 12 Houses of a Horoscope Chart

A preliminary introduction in the interpretation of the effects of 9 planets in the 12 houses of a birth chart/*janam kundali* is being taken up next by simple examples.

1st House (ascendant)

a. The sign of the ascendant in the birth chart needs to be noted. This sign confers special characteristics and fortune to a person as outlined in Chapter III, pages 27 to 29.
b. The location of the lord of the ascendant needs to be taken note of and its effects interpreted in terms of Chapter IV, pages 30 to 41.
c. The sign together with the placement of the lord of the ascendant is extremely important.

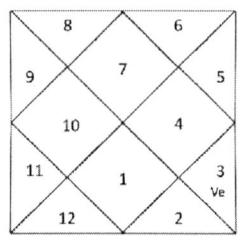

Example:

In this chart, the sign of ascendant is Libra and its lord is Venus which is located in 9th house, i.e. *Mooi-Trikon*. Such a placement would make the person extremely fortunate. 9th house, as we know, represents fortune, religion, father etc. Person would be highly talented, artistic and comfort loving and have a luxurious life style as these are the characteristics of Venus. Person would have great help and support from father and enjoy a very high status in life.

2nd House

d. The sign of 2nd house and the location of the lord of this sign is taken note of and the results interpreted in terms of chapter IV, pages 30 to 41.

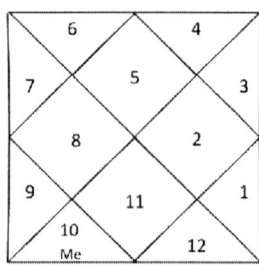

Example:

The sign of 2nd house in this chart is Virgo and its lord Mercury is located in 6th house in sign Capricorn. Since 6th house is the house of enemies, yet Capricorn is a friendly sign for Mercury, therefore, the effects of Mercury on 2nd house would be mixed. 2nd house, as we know, represents wealth, clan, speech etc., therefore the mixed effects of Mercury placed in 6th house, on the 2nd house would be that the person would have average or above average wealth. Mercury makes one proficient in trade and business and speech and therefore the person would be clever in speech. Since 6th house represents enemies, the person may gain by litigation against his/her enemies.

e. One would also need to study the overall horoscope to see if any other planet is aspecting the 2nd house and 6th house and the interpretation given above would get accordingly modified.

3rd House
Example:

The sign of 3rd house in this chart is Capricorn (10) and its lord Saturn is located in 4th house (*kendra*) in sign Aquarius which is its own sign. 3rd house holds the portfolios of courage, bravery, spirit of enterprise, brothers and sisters and short travels etc.

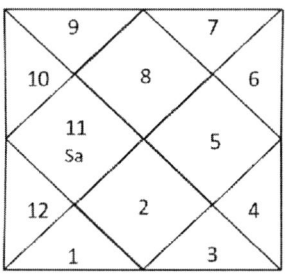

Saturn in Aquarius in 4th house (*kendra*) would be extremely helpful in respect of 3rd house. Therefore, such a person would be brave and courageous and would be very careful and calculating in enterprise as Saturn gives caution to a person. Person would undertake many pleasant journeys but have few brothers and sisters as Saturn gives sparse siblings.

4th House
Example:

The sign of 4th house in this chart is Pisces and its lord Jupiter is located in in 10th house (*kendra*) in sign Virgo (6). 4th house represents one's ancestral property, house, mother, happiness and vehicles etc. Thus, such a person would have excellent relations with mother as Jupiter aspects 4th house fully (its 7th aspect from 10th house). He/she would have a good house, enjoy ancestral property, have the use of many vehicles and would have happiness in life.

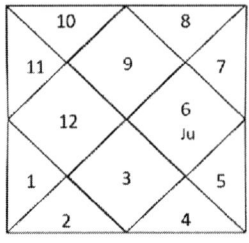

5th House
Example:

Here, sign of 5th house is Cancer (4) and its lord Moon is located in 10th house in sign Sagittarius (9) which is a friendly sign to it. Its effects would be that the person would have good education, beautiful and talented children, unexpected windfalls or gains from the government (10th house) would be loved by father and would probably have a government job.

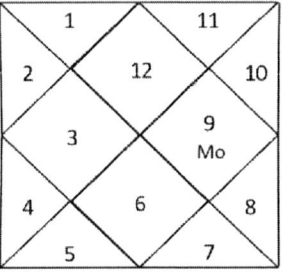

6th House
Example:

Here the sign of the 6th house is Gemini (3) and its lord Mercury located in 10th house in sign Libra (7). The effect would be that the person would have few enemies but they would be highly influential and connected with the government. His relations with father would

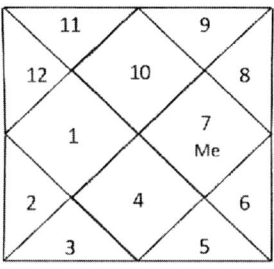

be indifferent as Mercury is lord of 6th house, which is the house of enemies, which is bad for the person, but Mercury is also the lord of the 9th house, i.e. the house of good fortune. Hence the overall effects of Mercury in respect of 10th house, i.e., government and father, would be mixed.

7th House
Example:

Here the sign of 7th house is Scorpio (8) and its lord Mars is located in its own sign Scorpio in 7th house. The effect would be that the person would have a beautiful wife who would be passionate, which is one of the qualities of Mars, and have a strong personality. Person would

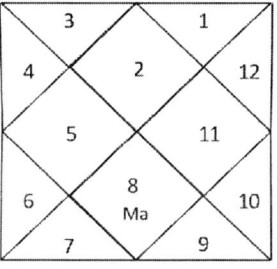

have good public relations and could have a successful partnership business.

8th House
Example:

Here, Scorpio is the sign in the 8th house and its lord Mars is located in its own sign Aries (1) in the 1st house (ascendant). Such a person would have a long life as 8th house is the lord of longevity. He would have good health and could have interests in archaeology and spirituality.

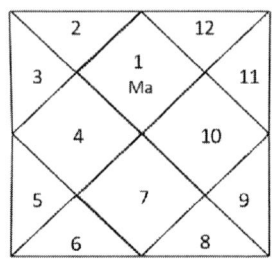

9th House
Example:

Here, Pisces (12) is the sign in the 9th house and its lord Jupiter is exalted in sign Cancer (4) in ascendant (House I) and it fully aspects 9th house (9th aspect). Such a person would be extremely lucky, would have a high moral character and would be spiritually minded, would have high reputation and perform many pilgrimages, journeys and travels by air.

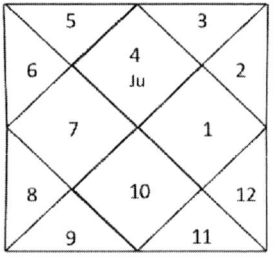

10th House
Example:

In this chart, Gemini (3) is the sign of 10th house and its lord Mercury is located in 11th house in sign Cancer (4). 10th house, as we know, is the lord of reputation, status, one's profession, one's relation with

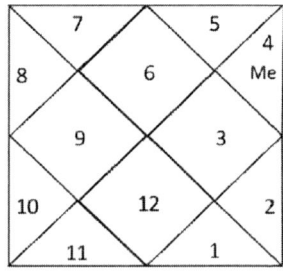

government and one's father. The effect would be that the person would enjoy a good reputation, have a high status, a highly paid government job and would have good relations with his/her father.

11th House
Example:

In this chart, sign of 11th house is Aquarius (11) and its lord Saturn is located in its own sign in that house. Now, 11th house represents gains, income, salary, good acts, vehicles etc. Therefore, such a person would have a high income from a government job as Saturn is also the lord of 10th

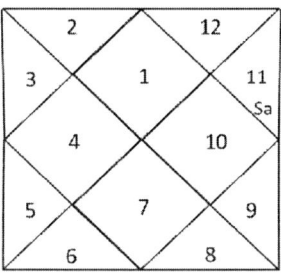

house in this chart which represents government and father etc. Person would have excellent relations with father and bring good fortune to father.

12th House
Example:

In this chart, the sign of 12th house is Pisces (12) and its ruler Jupiter is located in Aquarius (11) in 11th house. Now, 12th house represents expenses, losses, worries, anxieties etc. Although this person would have high income on account of the placement of Jupiter in 11th house

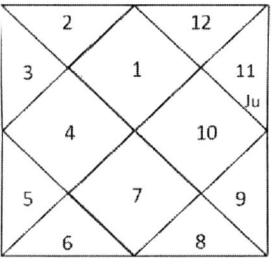

which is the house of income, he will also have high expenses and would not be able to save much money. Besides, such a person may also have many long journeys by air as 12th house also indicates journeys to foreign countries.

Detailed Systematic Assessment of the Twelve Houses of Horoscope Chart

When presented with a horoscope, an astrologer would study all the 12 houses of the various charts in detail before starting to make any predictions.

We are taking up a "sample horoscope", a *Janam Patri* or *Janamangam* or birth chart of a person for the purpose of illustrating how the detailed assessment of the twelve houses is carried out.

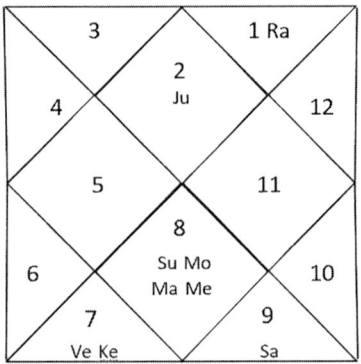

In the above horoscope chart, Taurus is the sign of the ascendant and Jupiter is placed in it. Venus and Ketu are placed in 6th house in sign Libra. Saturn is placed in 8th house in sign Sagittarius, Sun, Moon, Mars and Mercury are placed in 7th house in sign Scorpio and Rahu is placed in 12th house in sign Aries.

This is a very interesting horoscope.

General assessment of:
1st House or Ascendant:

1st house or Ascendant is the most important house in a horoscope. It indicates the physical and psychological make-up of a person. It also denotes the intelligence, potential/capacity, overall happiness and temperament of a person.

Since the sign in the 1st house is Taurus, the person would have the characteristics of sign Taurus, i.e. the person would be fair in complexion, lady-like in habits, would be fond of self-decoration, would be sweet of tongue, have many talents and virtues, would be intelligent, wise, have a stable personality and would have a remarkable equipoise and a "cool" temperament, could be argumentative, be devoted to family and have a long life. Since, Jupiter, which is the most benefic of all planets, is placed in 1st house, it would confer many beneficial effects on the person. However, since Jupiter happens to be in sign Taurus which is an inimical sign to it, its beneficial effects would be diminished by at least fifty percent.

However, since Jupiter, is fully aspected by Moon in the 7th house which not only gives a lot of strength to it but it also constitutes "*Gaj Kesri* Yoga", one of the very powerful Raj Yogas, the overall beneficial effects of Jupiter would be at least 75% of its total strength. Thus the person would enjoy good health, have a long life, would be a popular figure in public and would be rich and powerful. Lord of ascendant (sign 2) is Venus and it is placed in Libra which is its own sign (7) and is therefore powerful. However, it is located in the 6th house which is the house of enemies. This means that the person would have strong and powerful enemies throughout his life and would face a lot of competition and opposition; however, he would be successful in the majority of time in the struggle and strife of life. Furthermore, the ascendant is aspected by 4 planets from the 7th house; 7th house being a Kendra and the house of public relations, spouse, partnerships etc., it means that the person would remain in limelight throughout his life.

2nd House

2nd house is the house of wealth, one's bank balance, ancestry, power of speech and side business. The sign of 2nd house is Gemini (3) and it is empty. The lord of this house is Mercury and it is located in 7th house which is one of the

Kendras and it is in sign Scorpio (8) which is a neutral sign for it. Overall, the effects of Mercury on this house would be quite good. He would be wealthy, would have good command of speech, good skill in writing as Mercury confers literary skills and have very prominent and well-known ancestry. This house is blank or without any planet which is a good thing in itself. However, it is aspected by Mars in sign Scorpio, its own sign, from 7th house and Gemini is a neutral sign for Mars; therefore, the effect of Mars on the 2nd house would be good in respect of the portfolios of this house. Mars in Scorpio, its own house, is very powerful and it would impart a lot of impetus and energy to the 2nd house which it aspects fully from the 7th house by its special 8th aspect.

3rd House

3rd house shows one's courage, stamina, perseverance, one's brothers and sisters, ears, arms and short journeys. The sign of 3rd house is Cancer (4) and its lord Moon is located in 7th house. Moon is debilitated in sign Scorpio; however, its debilitation is neutralised by the presence of the lord of 7th house, Mars, in it. Another mitigating factor in neutralizing the debilitation of Moon is the 7th aspect of Jupiter from the 1st house on it. Thus the overall effects of Moon on the 3td house would be quite good. This means that the person would have a large number of siblings, would have good stamina and perform multiple short journeys throughout his life.

4th House

4th house represents one's house, landed property, one's mother, one's heart and emotions and happiness. The sign of this house is Leo (5) and it is blank or empty. Its lord is Sun, which is located in the 7th house in sign Scorpio. Now 7th house is one of the *Kendras* and Scorpio is a friendly sign for Sun. Therefore, the effects of Sun on this house would be excellent. He would have a nice house or more than one house, would enjoy a lot of ancestral property, would have a doting and somewhat domineering mother as Sun, the lord of this house has a fiery temperament. The degree of happiness in life would be somewhat diluted by the fiery nature of the lord of this house, namely, Sun.

5th House

5th house indicates one's intelligence, education, children, speech, fame, administrative acumen and windfalls. The sign of this house is Virgo (6) and this house is empty. The lord of this house Mercury is located in 7th

house in sign Scorpio which is a neutral sign for this planet. Further, this house is aspected fully by Jupiter in the 1st house, i.e. the 5th *drishti* of Jupiter. Mercury is the lord of occult sciences, of writing, literature, of intelligence, of mathematics and Jupiter is the lord of intelligence, all fields of education, spirituality and literature. This house would enjoy all the combined positive effects of Mercury and Jupiter.

Therefore, he would be highly intelligent, would be highly educated and qualified, a literary person, a scholar and an authority on some aspect of literature. He would be very famous and known throughout the length and breadth of the land. He would also be awarded some titles for his outstanding contributions to literature and original creative writing.

6th House

6th house gives an idea of one's enemies, illnesses, anxieties, litigations, debts and doubts. The sign of 6th house is Libra (7) and its lord Venus is placed in it. Ketu is also placed in this house. Normally when a planet is placed in its own sign, it gives excellent effects; however, since this is the house of enemies, illnesses and other negative things, the good effects of Venus are diminished to some extent. The presence of Ketu in this house means that his enemies would be destroyed. Despite the fact that he would have many enemies who would be highly educated, influential and powerful, he would nearly always vanquish them. Person would face tough competitions in his career throughout his life but because of Ketu he would emerge as "victor" nearly every time. Besides, we have already made a reference to the fact that the presence of Jupiter in a Kendra and particularly so in the ascendant as in this case, removes numerous "*doshas*" or afflictions in the horoscope of a person.

7th House

7th house tells us about married life of a person, the spouse, relationship with partner, one's business particularly "partnership business", cause of death etc. Sign of 7th house is Scorpio (8) and its lord Mars is positioned here. Since 7th house is a Kendra and its lord is present here, it becomes the most important house of this horoscope. Thus, he would have a long and happy married life. Besides that, three other major planets including Sun, Moon and Mercury are also placed in this house. Sun is again very powerful in this house as it is in the friendly sign of Scorpio. Although Moon is debilitated in Scorpio sign, it is in conjunction with the lord of the house, namely, Mars. This would have the effect of neutralizing the debilitation of Moon; as a result, Moon would become a helpful planet for this house. Mercury is also present in this house and the sign Scorpio is neutral for it; since Mercury is again in conjunction with the lord of this house (Mars), it would also have an overall good effect on this house. As a result of the combined strength of 4 planets and the direct aspect of Jupiter from ascendant on this house, the person would be a very famous public figure known throughout the land for his meritorious and virtuous character. His counsel would be sought after by the highest in the land including the head of the State.

8th House

8th house represents longevity, death, mental anxieties, obstacles, fractures and surgical operations, espionage, archaeological interests, one's in-laws etc.

Saturn is placed in this house and it gives longevity to the person. The sign of 8th house is Sagittarius and this is inimical to Saturn. Therefore, it would cause some problems in this house. For instance, the person could suffer a fracture in childhood with some complications.

He may undergo several surgical operations during the course of his life. Since, Jupiter is the lord of this house and it is placed in ascendant, it would grant longevity to the person and a relatively healthy and disease-free life. Person would face several hardships and difficult times during the prevalence of *Mahadasha* of Saturn and also in its *Antardasha* during the *Mahadasha* of other planets. Mercury and Mars being the lords of 2nd and 7th house respectively are the "*markesh*" planets, i.e. the cause of death in this horoscope.

9th House

9th house indicates one's fortune or luck, spiritual inclination, happiness from father, windfalls or unexpected gains and short journeys by air.

Sign of the 9th house is Capricorn and its lord Saturn is located in the 8th house in its inimical sign Sagittarius. Therefore, the effects of Saturn on this house would be negative. However, this house is fully aspected by a powerful Jupiter in the ascendant by its 9th drishti. That would have a strong positive effect on this house and mitigate the ill-effects of Saturn. Thus, the person would have a fairly good fortune and would be somewhat spiritually inclined.

10th House

10th house indicates one's profession, business, relation with government, public reputation, social prestige, fame, influence, authority and one's father. The sign of 10th house is Aquarius (11) and its lord Saturn is positioned in 8th house in sign Sagittarius which is an inimical sign for it. Therefore, Saturn is not very helpful for this house. However, Saturn does aspect the 10th house fully with its 3rd *drishti* or 3rd aspect. This house is also aspected fully by a very powerful Mars in the 7th house (*Kendra*) by its 4th *drishti* or 4th aspect. The combined effect of 2 planets fully aspecting this house would be that he would be able to achieve a good position in government service but may not be able to continue for long time in that position due to a weak lord of 10th house, i.e. Saturn. However, he would continue to enjoy a good name and reputation in government circles. His father would have a high social status.

11th House

11th house represents one's income, gains, luxuries, good acts, vehicles, wealth etc. The sign of 11th house is Pisces (12) and its lord Jupiter is placed in the ascendant – the most important Kendra. Besides, some regular personal pension, the person would gain income through his literary works, advisory functions, authorship of books, winning of awards and teaching activities and chairmanship of social organisations.

12th House

12th house indicates one's losses, expenses, illnesses, worries, anxieties, charity etc.

The sign of 12th house is Aries (1) and it is occupied by Rahu. Its lord Mars is placed in its own sign in the 7th house which is a Kendra. The placement of Rahu in this house is somewhat controversial in its effects. Some regard it as harmful causing illness and increasing enemies and loss of income. Others regard it not so harmful and believe that it tends to destroy enemies by its 7th aspect on 6th house and makes the person undertake some trips to foreign lands. The effect of lordship of this house by a powerful Mars would tend to accentuate his anxieties and may even be conducive to an agitated state of mind.

2. Lunar Chart or *Chander Kundli* of the same person.

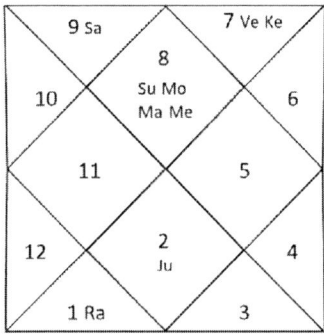

Lunar chart or *Chander Kundli* (CK) is an important chart and it should be seen after the *Janam Kundli* (JK) has been assessed. All the 12 houses are assessed individually in CK as in J.K. When CK supports the findings of the birth chart (JK), the latter get reinforced. If the findings of the lunar chart are in conflict in any respect with those of the birth chart (JK), the latter need to be modified accordingly. Sometimes lunar chart may bring out a new finding which was not revealed in the birth chart; these have to be included in the overall prediction. These are finer nuances of astrology and an experienced astrologer would be able to evaluate them appropriately.

Dasha/Antardasha or Reigning Period of Planets in the Life of an Individual

Birth constellation or "*Janam Nakshtrya*" that is prevailing at the time of birth of a person can be easily found out by referring to the almanac/*Jantri*. Each Nakshtrya lasts for a certain period-of time and the *Jantri*/almanac will tell how much of its time it has already spent and how much of its time remains to be spent at the time of birth of the person. Each *Nakshtrya* has a ruling planet and this has been described earlier. If, for example, a child is born when *Punarvasu Nakshtrya* is prevailing, we can easily find by referring to the relevant Table (page 49) that the lord of this *Nakshtrya* is Jupiter. This means that Jupiter is the ruling (reigning) planet of that child at the time of birth. We know that span of reign of Jupiter is 16 years. **The span of reign of a planet is called "*Dasha*" in astrological language**. In the instant case, almanac indicates that the *Punarvasu Nakshtrya* had spent half of its span at the time of birth of the child; it means that, out of its overall span of 16 years, Jupiter still has half of its overall time of 16 years left over when the child was born. Half of the total of 16 years amounts to eight years (See Table below). We can, therefore, say that this particular child was born in the *Mahadasha* of Jupiter which still had 8 years' time left to complete its term. "*Maha*" means major. **The astrological system describing the major spans of the reign of 9 planets is called "*Vishontri Mahadasha*".**

The *Mahadasha* of planets occurs in a well-defined sequence.

Table showing the chronological sequence of *Mahadasha* of 9 planets and their duration starting with planet Sun

Serial Number	Planet	Period
1	Sun	6years
2	Moon	10years
3	Mars	7years
4	Rahu	18years
5	Jupiter	16years
6	Saturn	19years
7	Mercury	17years
8	Ketu	7years
9	Venus	20years

The sequence of *Mahadasha* starts from the planet in whose *Mahadasha* one is born. In the instant case, the child was born in the *Mahadasha* of Jupiter and had 8 years of the

Mahadasha of Jupiter yet left over to complete its reign. The sequence of *Mahadashas* to follow after completion of the *Mahadasha* of Jupiter would be: Saturn, Mercury, Ketu, Venus, Sun, Moon, Mars and Rahu in that order.

Let us take another example to illustrate the sequence: Suppose a child is born in the *Mahadasha* of Sun, the next *Mahadasha* in the sequence would be that of Moon and that would be followed by those of Mars, Rahu, Jupiter, Saturn, Mercury, Ketu and finally that of Venus in that order.

Antardasha or Subperiod of Planets During the Operation of *Mahadasha*

During the course of *Mahadasha* (major reign) of a planet, other 8 planets also become active in a well-defined sequence for a specified period of time. This sub-period of activity of other planets during the *Mahadasha* of a planet is referred to as "*Antardasha*". For example, as shown in the Table below, during the 16 years of *Mahadasha* of Jupiter, the first subperiod/*antardasha* is that of Jupiter itself and it lasts for 2 years, 1 month and 18 days. This is spoken of as "*Antardasha* of Jupiter in the *Mahadasha* of Jupiter" or more simply expressed as "Jupiter in Jupiter". The *Antardasha* of other planets occurs in the same sequence as is the case with *Mahadasha*. Thus during the *Mahadasha* of Jupiter, the *Antardasha* of Jupiter is followed by that of Saturn, Mercury, Ketu, Venus, Sun, Mars and finally that of Rahu in that order. These *Antardashas* are worked out mathematically by an astrologer and are shown in the horoscope chart of a person.

Significance of *Mahadasha* and *Antardasha*

When a planet is running its *Mahadasha*, i.e. in its own reign, it would enjoy maximum power and show its effects fully. These effects get modified by the influence of the planet of *antardasha*. If *Antardasha* planet is friendly to *Mahadasha* planet, it would potentiate the effects of the *Mahadasha* planet; if it is unfriendly or inimical planet, it would dilute/diminish the effects of *Mahadasha* planet. If the *Antardasha* planet is neutral to *Mahadasha* planet, it would not alter the effects of *Mahadasha* planet; if the *Antardasha* planet is the same as the *Mahadasha* planet, then it would significantly enhance the effects of the *Mahadasha* planet. For example, during the *Mahadasha* of Jupiter, there is *Antardasha* of Jupiter for 2 years, 1month and 18. During this period, Jupiter would show its maximum beneficial effects.

Tables showing the periods of *Antardasha* of planets during the course of the prevalence of *Vishontri Mahadasha* of a Planet are set forth below. This information would greatly facilitate the task of making predictions.

Antardasha of 9 planets during *Vishontri Mahadasha* of Mars.

Planets	Period of *Antardasha*
Mars	4 months and 27days
Rahu	1 year and 18 days
Jupiter	11 months and 6 days
Saturn	1 year,1 month and 9
Mercury	11 months and 27 days
Ketu	4 months and 27 days
Venus	1 year, 2months
Sun	4 months and 6 days
Moon	7 months

Antardasha of 9 planets during the *Vishontri Mahadasha* of Rahu

Planets	Period of *Antardasha*
Rahu	2 years, 8 months and 12 Days
Jupiter	2 years, 4 months and 24Days
Saturn	2 years,10 months and 6 days
Mercury	2 years, 6 months and 18 Days
Ketu	1 year and 18 days
Venus	3 years
Sun	10 months and 24 days
Moon	1 year and 6 months
Mars	1 year and 18 days

Antardasha of 9 planets during *Vishontri Mahadasha* of Jupiter

Planet	Period of *Antardasha*
Jupiter	2 years, 1month and 18 days
Saturn	2 years, 6 months and 12 days
Mercury	2 years, 3 months and 6 days
Ketu	11 months and 6 days
Venus	2 years and 8 months
Sun	9 months and 18 days
Moon	1year and 4 months
Mars	1year and 4 months
Rahu	2 years 4 months and 27 days

Antardasha of 9 planets during the *Vishontri Mahadasha* of Saturn

Planet	Period of *Antardasha*
Saturn	3 years and 3 days
Mercury	2 years, 8 months and 9 days
Ketu	1 year, 1 month and 9 days
Venus	3 years and 2 months
Sun	11 months and 12 days
Moon	1 year and 7 months
Mars	1 year, 1 month and 9 days
Rahu	2 years, 10 months and 6 days
Jupiter	2 years, 6 months and 12 days

Antardasha of 9 planets during the *Vishontri Mahadasha* of Mercury

Planet	Period of *Antardasha*
Mercury	2 years, 4 months and 27 days
Ketu	11 months and 27 days
Venus	2 years and 10 months
Sun	10 months and 6 days
Moon	1 year and 5 months
Mars	11 months and 27 days
Rahu	2 years, 6 months and 18 days
Jupiter	2 years, 3 months and 6 days
Saturn	2 years, 8 months and 9 days

Antardasha of 9 planets during *Vishontri Mahadasha* of Ketu

Planet	Period of *Antardasha*
Ketu	4 months and 27 days
Venus	1 year and 2 months
Sun	4 months and 6 days
Moon	7 months
Mars	4 months and 27 days
Rahu	1 year and 18 days
Jupiter	11 months and 6 days
Saturn	1 year, 1 month and 9 days
Mercury	11 months and 27 days

Antardasha of 9 planets during *Vishontri Mahadasha* of Venus

Planet	Period of Antardasha
Venus	3 years and 4 months
Sun	1 year
Moon	1 year and 8 months
Mars	1 year and 2 months
Rahu	3 years
Jupiter	2 years and 8 months
Saturn	3 years and 2 months
Mercury	2 years and 10 months
Ketu	1 year and 2 months

Antardasha of 9 planets during the *Vishontri Mahadasha* of Sun

Planet	Period of *Antardasha*
Sun	3 months and 18 days
Moon	6 months
Mars	4 months and 6 days
Rahu	10 months and 24 days
Jupiter	9 months and 18 days
Saturn	11 months and 12 days
Mercury	10 months and 6 days
Ketu	4 months and 6 days
Venus	12 months

Antardasha of 9 planets during *Vishontri Mahadasha* of Moon

Planet	Period of *Antardasha*
Moon	10 months
Mars	7 months
Rahu	1 year and 6 months
Jupiter	1 year and 4 months
Saturn	1 year and 7 months
Mercury	1 year and 5 months
Ketu	7 months
Venus	1 year and 8 months
Sun	6 months

Prayantradasha in *Antardasha*

Just as we studied *Antardasha* in *Mahadasha*, in a similar manner, there is further refinement in *Antardasha* of a planet in having its *Prayantradasha*. This is worked out by mathematical calculations in an exercise similar to the one carried out in working out the periods of *Antardasha* during

Mahadasha. For example, during the 19 years of *Vishontri Mahadasha* of Saturn, there is *Antardasha* of Saturn (see Table on page 114) for a period of 3 years and 3 months. Now, during the reign of this sub-period or *Antardasha* of Saturn, all the 9 planets run their course in the standard sequence, which in this case would be: Saturn, Mercury, Ketu, Venus, Sun, Moon, Mars, Rahu and Jupiter. And each of them would have their short period of reign. This period of reign of a planet during the *Antardasha* of a planet is referred to as "*Prayantradasha*". The period of *Prayantradasha* of a planet is usually a brief one, amounting to a few days or weeks. This would provide more detailed and minute information and thus greatly enhance the quality of making more precise predictions from day to day. *Prayantradasha* is worked out by the professional astrologer at the time of preparing the horoscope chart.

Thus the *Prayantradasha* of Saturn would run in the following sequence:

Planet	Period of *Prayantradasha*
Saturn	6 months and 6 days
Mercury	5 months and 16 days
Ketu	2 months and 9 days
Venus	6 months and 16 days
Sun	1 month and 29 days
Moon	3 months and 13 days
Mars	2 months and 9 days
Rahu	5 months and 11 days
Jupiter	5 months and 7 days

Prayantradashas of other planets can be worked out in a similar manner using the standard calculation chart. This, as stated earlier, is usually prepared by the professional astrologer at the time of preparing the horoscope of a person. When this is available, it greatly enhances the quality of detailed prediction in terms of days and weeks.

Miscellaneous Issues:
(a) Answering questions by *Prashna Kundli* (PK) or *Gochar Kundli* (GK)
(b) Matching Horoscopes.
(c) My today.

Answering Questions by *Prashna Kundli*
Example
Supposing someone asks the practitioner/predictor at 1625 hours on 8th May 2018 at Jammu, India, regarding the result/outcome of an examination that he has appeared in recently. A *Gochar Kundli* at the time of asking the question is prepared by referring to the "*lagan sarni*" in *Panchang*. The *Gochar Kundli* (GK) is also known as "*Prashna Kundli*" (PK).

It is a basic principle of astrology that the ascendant or lagna must always be looked at first for making any prediction, even for making a simple prediction like an examination result. If the ascendant in the *Prashan Kundli* (PK) is strong, it indicates a positive outcome; if the ascendant is weak, it indicates an unfavourable outcome. In addition to the ascendant, the 5th house which 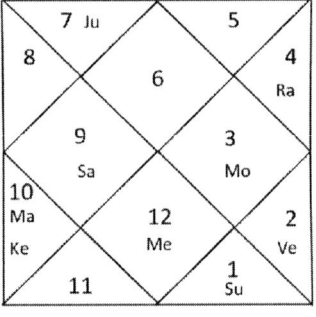 is the house of education and the 9th house which is the house of fortune, need to be considered for answering the question.

Sign of 5th house in GK is Capricorn (10) and its lord, Saturn, is located in 4th house (Kendra) in an unfriendly sign Sagittarius (9). Saturn in 4th house (Kendra) is strong but being in the unfriendly sign Sagittarius makes it somewhat weak. However, an exalted Mars in sign Capricorn is located in 5th house which makes this house very strong. That indicates a brilliant outcome of the examination.

Now, sign of 9th house in GK is Taurus and its lord, Venus, is located in this house in its own sign. This indicates an extremely favourable outcome.

Sign of ascendant in GK is Virgo and its lord Mercury is located in 7th house which is a Kendra and it fully aspects the ascendant with its 7th *drishti*. However, Mercury is debilitated in sign Pisces (12) in 7th house making it considerably weak Since, Mercury fully aspects the ascendant in Virgo sign where it gets exalted, the overall effect would be positive.

Overall, out of the three parameters considered for answering the question, the outcome of two parameters is brilliant and a positive outcome for the third parameter. Therefore, one can unhesitatingly predict that the person would have a brilliant success in the examination.

Matching Horoscopes of Boy and Girl for Matrimony

A standard *Panchang/Jantri contains* a Table in which the *Nakshtryas* with their 4 *charans* and the lunar sign/*Rashi* of the boy at the time of his birth is drawn on one side and the *Nakshtryas* and the lunar sign/*Rashi** of the girl is drawn across the boy's data. The point where the boy's data meet/intersect the girl's data in the Table would indicate the "points score" of matching the boys' and girls' horoscopes for matrimony. The score can range from a minimum of 2 to a maximum of 36. For example, if a boy is born in Aries sign, in *charan* 3 of *Asshwini Nakshtryas* and the girl is born in Gemini sign, in *charan* 4 of *Mrigshar Nakshtryas*, reference to the Table shows that the points score at the intersection of the two data is 26. Usually, a score of more than 18 points/*gunas*+ is said to denote a "good match", i.e. the marriage would be auspicious and happy. If the points/*gunas* are less than 18, then such a marriage should preferably be avoided. Besides the points, there are also eight defects/*doshas* in the matching process which need to be considered for the final verdict on the matching of horoscopes. These are: (1) *Varan*, (2) *Vashya*, (3) Tara, (4)

Yoni, (5) *Grahamaitri*, (6) *Ganmaitri* (7) *Bhakoot* and (8) *Nadi*.

These are carefully evaluated by a professional astrologer before the final verdict on the prospects of harmonious relationship between the boy and the girl in the matching process is pronounced.

Moon sign is called the *Rashi** of a person.
Gunas+ means the points scored for harmonious relationship.

My Today

All of us experience that all days are not alike. Some days are bright and happy; they start on a happy note, progress smoothly in a problem-free manner and end on a cheerful and happy note. Clearly, there are many components to a day and the experience varies from day-to-day and person to person. Does the planetary influence have a role in shaping the trend and tenor of a day? It seems that this indeed is the case. Fundamentally, there are two principal components of a day, one's work and one's state of mind. It may be noted that Moon is the fastest moving among the 9 planets and it stays in a sign for approximately two and a half days. *Nakshtrya* changes every day and we have new *Nakshtrya* every day. *Nakshtrya* of the day determines the tenor and complexion of the day in so far as one's work, profession or business is concerned. Other planets move much more slowly and they too broadly influence the general pattern of one's life during the period of their reign or *dasha*.

However, their influence on the day-to-day minute events in one's life is not as dramatic or noticeable. A look at the *Panchang/Jantri* would clearly show the prevailing *Nakshtrya* of the day and also the Moon sign of the day and their duration. Each *Nakshtrya* has a specific planet (see Table below) as its lord and that planet would determine the complexion and trend of one's work or business on that day. The second factor is the sign and house of placement of Moon on a given day and that would determine the "state of one's mind" on that day. Moon, represents the mind and indicates whether one is going to be happy and cheerful or sad and unhappy or in an indifferent mood depending upon its sign and placement.

Zodiacal Sign	*Nakshtry*a in that Sign	**Ruling Planet**
Aries	4 *charans* of *Ashwini*, 4 *charans* of *Bharni* and 1st *charan* of *Kritka*	Mars
Taurus	3 *charans* of *Kritka*, 4 *charans* of *Rohini* and 2 *charans* of Mrigshira	Venus
Gemini	Last 2 *charans* of *Mrigshira*, 4 *charans* of *Ardra* and 1st three *charans* of *Punarvasu*	Mercury
Taurus	Last *charan* of *Punarvasu*, 4 *charans* of *Pushya* and 4 *charans* of *Aashlesha*	Moon
Leo	4 *charans* of *Magha*, 4 *charans* of *Purva-Phalguni* and 1st *charan* of *Uttar-Phalguni*	Sun
Virgo	Last 3 *charans* of *Uttar Phalguni*, 4 *charans* of *Hasta* and the 1st 2 *charans* of *Chitra*	Mercury

Libra	Last 2 *charans* of *Chitra*, 4 *charans* of Swati and the 1st 3 *charans* of *Vishaka*	Venus
Scorpio	Last *charan* of *Vishaka*, 4 *charans* of *Anuradha* and 4 *charans* of *yeshta*	Mars
Sagittarius	4 *charans* of *Moola*, 4 *charans* of *Purva-Khara* and the 1st *charan* of *Uttar-Khara*	Jupiter
Capricorn	Last 3 *charans* of *Uttar-Khara*, 4 *charans* of *Shravan* and 1st 2 *charans* of *Dhanishta*	Saturn
Aquarius	Last 2 *charans* of *Dhanishta*, 4 *charans* of *Shatbhaka* and 1st 3 *charans* of *Purva-Bhadarpad*	Saturn
Pisces	Last *charan* of *Purva-Bhadarpad*, 4 *charans* of *Uttarbhadarpad* and 4 *charans* of *Revti*	Jupiter

Nakshtrya

Nakshtrya of the day is found out by referring to *Panchang/Jantri* and its lord can be known by referring to the above chart. Next step is to have a look at the birth chart or *Lagna Kundli* (LK) of the person in order to see the sign of the ascendant. The planet ruling the sign of the ascendant of the person in the *Gochar Kundli* (GK) would determine the kind of day the person would have regarding his work or profession. This is being illustrated by an example.

Example

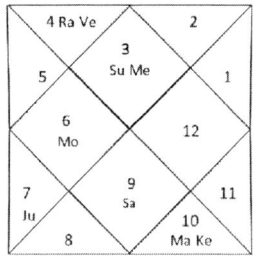

Gochar Kundli (GK) on 22/06/18

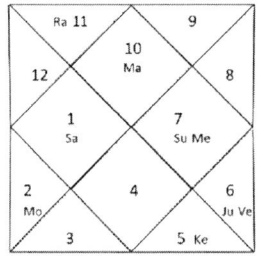

Native Chart or Janam Kundli (JK) of the person.

Nakshtrya on 22/06/2018 is *Chitra* as found out from *Panchang* and its lord is Mars. Now, Mars on that day happens to be located in sign Capricorn (10), which is the sign of its exaltation. Since Capricorn (10) happens to be the sign of the ascendant of the person in his native chart or JK, its lord, the exalted Mars would influence that day in so far as his work or business is concerned. Since ascendant represents the portfolios of overall well-being, prosperity, prestige and status of a person, we can confidently and unhesitatingly predict that the person would have an excellent day from the work and business point of view.

MOON

We find that Moon is placed in sign Virgo in *Gochar* chart and it is in sign Taurus (2) in the native chart or JK. The relationship of Moon in JK and GK, i.e. between Taurus and Virgo is 5th/9th*[*], i.e. Moon sign of the day is 5th from Moon sign in native chart or JK. This 5th/9th relationship of Moon is highly auspicious and therefore, we can safely predict that the person would be very happy and on top of the world on that day.

---

*The house of location of Moon in native chart (JK) is counted as number 1 for the purpose of calculating the relationship of Gochar Moon and native Moon and vice versa.

Native Moon	Gochar Moon	Relationship between native Moon and Gochar Moon	Effects on the State of Mind
4	4	1	Material gain and an occasion to celebrate
4	5	2nd	Happy state of mind from gain in business
4	6	3rd	Positive state of mind, gain from brother
4	7	4th	Unhappiness, quarrels and arguments and unnecessary and wasteful travel
4	8	5th	Comfortable state of mind, average gain
4	9	6th	Anxiety and worry: fear from enemy, quarrels and argumentation

4	10	7th	Happiness: good for business and happiness from spouse
4	11	8th	Miserable: obstacles in all undertakings
4	12	9th	Happy state of mind: fulfilment of desire
4	1	10th	Happiness: profit from business and benefit from government
4	2	11th	Great happiness from fulfilment of desire and gains
4	3	12th	Sadness and disappointment: unexpected loss and unnecessary and wasteful travel

Please note that the numerals have been used to denote the Moon sign for simplicity.

Please note that for the purpose of simplification, illustrating the underlying principle, sign 2 or Taurus has been used for the native Moon. From the example, it should be simple for one to work out the relationship of Moon in any native chart with the *Gochar* Moon of the day.

Number 1 stands for Aries; Number 2 stands for Taurus; Number 3 stands for Gemini; Number 4 stands for Cancer; Number 5 stands for Leo; Number 6 stands for Virgo: Number 7 stands for Libra; Number 8 stands for Scorpio; Number 9 stands for Sagittarius; Number 10 stands for Capricorn; Number 11 stands for Aquarius and Number 12 stands for Pisces.

Some Illustrating Horoscopes

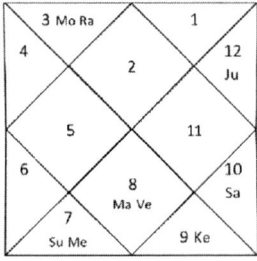

Lagan Kundli (LK) of a person.

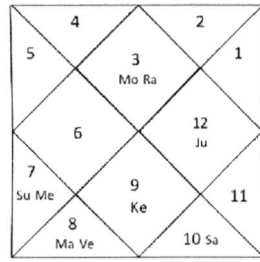

Chander Kundli (CK) of the same person.

In this section, correlating Lagan Kundli (LK), *Chander Kundli* (CK) and *Navamsh Kundli (NK)* is being taken up in order to illustrate the effects produced on the overall prediction by this exercise. Whereas, it is useful to remember that LK remains the most important chart in the task of making predictions, such predictions need to be tempered with the simultaneous consideration of CK and NK. Such an exercise would yield a more comprehensive perspective on the nuances of the art of astrology.

Top of this page shows 2 charts, *Lagan Kundli* (LK) and *Chander Kundli* (CK) of a person. Correlating these 2 charts would bring out the value of the exercise.

1st House

In *Janam Kundli* (JK) the sign in Ascendant (1st house) is Taurus (2) and its lord is Venus and that is located in the 7th house in sign Scorpio. Venus is quite powerful in this house for a number of reasons. (1) 7th house is a Kendra, (2) the sign of the 7th house is Scorpio and its lord Mars is located here, (3) Jupiter is located in 11th house in its own sign Pisces and it directly aspects Venus in the 7th house by its 9th aspect (*drishti*) and (4) Venus in 7th house is in sign Scorpio which is a neutral sign for it, therefore Venus is quite powerful in this house.

From the 7th house, a powerful Venus looks at ascendant fully by its 7th aspect. The effects of Venus on ascendant would be that the person would be handsome, strong and would have a long life.

In *chander kundli* (CK) the sign in the 1st house is Gemini (3) and its lord Mercury is located in the friendly sign of Libra (7) in the 5th house. 5th house is the house of education, children, windfalls, fame etc. Therefore, the person would be lucky, have good education, good children and would be rich.

In this correlation, the predictive effects of birth LK and CK are positive and support each other. It can thus be predicted unhesitatingly that such a person would have a handsome personality, would be highly educated, would have a lot of friends, (effects of Venus in 7th house), would enjoy good health and have a long life.

2nd House

In Lagan *Kundli* (LK), Rahu and Moon are located in 2nd house in sign Gemini. The lord of Gemini is Mercury which is located in 6th house in the friendly sign, Libra.

6th house is the house of enemies and though Mercury is in the friendly sign Libra, it considerably loses its strength by virtue of its being placed in the 6th house. Moon and Rahu are unfriendly to each other by temperament. Moon, which represents the mind is quite uncomfortable here in the company of Rahu. Nature of Rahu is very different than that of Moon. Rahu is impatient, hasty and prone to taking wrong decisions. However, Rahu is exalted in sign Gemini in 2nd house. 2nd house represents wealth, clan, speech etc. The effect of conjunction of Rahu and Moon in this house would be that the person would have two distinct strands of mutually conflicting thought currents in his mind and would often be confused. However, he would be wealthy as Rahu is exalted in this house. His speech would vary from time to time depending on whether Moon or Rahu is dominating at a given point in time. Sometimes he would be very soft-spoken, cheerful and smiling and at other times, he would be abrupt and harsh in speech.

In the *Chander Kundli* (CK), the lord of 2nd house is Moon which is located in the 1st house. This is a favourable location for Moon and indicates that such a person would have a lovely voice, would be very rich, have a large clan and would be very pleasant, well-mannered, charming and sophisticated. Since the 2nd house is much stronger in CK than in LK, overall, the effects of CK would prevail over those of JK.

3rd House

Sign of 3rd house in Lagan *Kundli* (LK) is Cancer and its lord Moon is located in its neutral sign, Gemini in 2nd house and is afflicted by Rahu. 3rd house represents courage, bravery, initiative, siblings, short travels etc. His initiative, drive and courage (portfolios of 3rd house) would be generally good but at times he would feel discouraged and depressed because of affliction of Moon by Rahu. He would have few siblings (portfolio of 3rd house) but would travel a lot as Rahu and Moon are both fond of travelling.

In *Chander Kundli* (CK), Leo, is the sign of 3rd house and its lord, Sun, is debilitated and is located in 5th house. A planet in 5th house usually gives positive results. However, since Sun is debilitated here, its effects on the 3rd house would be mixed. Although it is in Sun's nature to give courage, incentive and bravery, yet because of its debilitation, the person may get discouraged and depressed at times. His relations with siblings (portfolio of 3rd house) would again be mixed because of debilitated Sun in the 5th house. Overall, effect of LK and CK on the 3rd house would be mixed. Though he may start most things with good initiative and enthusiasm, he may get discouraged if positive results are not forthcoming immediately and would be somewhat lacking in quality of perseverance.

4th House

In JK, the sign in 4th house is Leo. Its lord Sun is located in 6th house, which is the house of enemies and is debilitated in sign Libra. Therefore, its effect on the 4th house would not be favourable. Since 4th house represents one's residential house, ancestral property, mother etc., the person may live away from the place of birth, may not enjoy ancestral property and may not have good relations with his mother.

In CK, the sign of 4th house is Virgo. Its lord Mercury is located in 5th house in sign Libra which is a friendly sign to it. Planets located in 5th house generally yield positive and beneficial effects. Its effects would be that the person would enjoy the benefits of ancestral property, would have many vehicles, would have a beautiful house of his own and would have very good relations with mother. Here, the good effects of CK would overweigh the ill-effects of JK. Overall, the planetary effects on the 4th house would be above average in their benefits.

5th House

In JK, the sign of 5th house is Virgo. Its lord, Mercury is located in 6th house in friendly sign Libra (7). 6th house is the house of enemies and location of Mercury in this house would give adverse effects to the 5th house of which it is the lord. However, since Mercury is in friendly sign of Libra, its bad effects would be mitigated to some extent. 5th house represents education, children, windfalls etc. This may result in the person losing a year or more in educational career and the person may be deprived of other benefits of 5th house such as children, windfalls, titles etc. However in JK, Jupiter is located in 11th house in its own sign, Pisces, and it fully aspects the 5th house by its 7th aspect or *drishti*. Thus, Jupiter would not only remove the ill-effects of Mercury by its full aspect on the 5th house, but also result in the person enjoying all the benefits of 5th house i.e. person would be highly qualified, would have at least one male child who would be very bright, would be famous, have good reputation and would be rich.

In CK, sign of 5th house is Libra. Its lord, Venus is located in 6th house in its neutral sign Scorpio in conjunction with Mars, the lord of this house. Although Venus would be somewhat weakened by its position in the 6th house, which is the house of enemies, but its conjunction with Mars – the lord of this house – would obviate that weakness and, in fact, make it reasonably strong. Further, debilitated Sun and a friendly Mercury are located in 5th house in sign Libra. Debilitated Sun in 5th house would produce a failure in studies, some bad name through an incident and some problem with the children in their birth. However, the location of friendly Mercury in this house would mitigate the ill effects of debilitated Sun and give positive effects on this house and the person would have high education, good reputation and good children. Taking into account the JK and CK together, their overall effects on the 5th house would be much above average and generally favourable.

6th House

In JK, the sign of 6th house is Libra. Its lord, Venus is located in 7th house in its neutral sign Scorpio. Besides, Sun and Mercury are located in sign Libra in this house. Sun is debilitated in this house in sign Libra but Mercury is in its friendly sign of Libra. Further, 6th house is aspected* fully by Saturn from 9th house by its 10th aspect or *drishti*. 6th house, as we know, is the house of enemies, litigation, disputes etc. Sun in the 6th house destroys the enemies even if it is debilitated. Mercury in the friendly sign Libra has a mixed effect on this house; it promotes enemies as well as destroys enemies. Saturn from 9th house completely routs enemies by its direct 10th aspect. The overall planetary effects on this house would be that person would have a few enemies because of Mercury but they would not be able to harm him; in fact, the enemies would be destroyed and routed so comprehensively and effectively that they would not dare oppose him and may, in fact, try to curry favour and friendship with him. Person could also gain through litigation.

In CK, sign of 6th house is Scorpio and its lord Mars is located here. Mars would again destroy his enemies. Jupiter from 10th house by its 9th aspect on 6th house may promote some enemies. However, the combined effects of JK and CK indicate that the person would invariably vanquish his enemies.

7th House

In JK, the sign of 7th house is Scorpio and its lord, Mars, is located here in its own sign. Venus is also located here in its neutral sign of Scorpio. Further, this house is fully aspected by Jupiter from 11th house by its 9th aspect. 7th house represents spouse, public relations, side-business etc. Mars in its own sign in this house would give him a beautiful and strong-willed spouse. Venus in 7th house gives rise to multiple affairs with members of opposite sex and delays marriage. Jupiter in the 11th house of gains, exerts an extremely beneficial effect on this house by its 9th aspect and removes all the ill-effects or afflictions caused by Venus. Person would have a happy married life despite the delay in marriage and would enjoy excellent public relations and could have a side business, besides his/her main profession.

In CK, the sign of 7th house is Sagittarius and its lord, Jupiter, is located in 10th house (Kendra) in its own sign. This is an extremely favourable indication for 7th house. Thus, the overall effects of JK and CK would be highly favourable for this house.

8th House

In JK, sign of 8th house is Sagittarius and Ketu is located in it and is exalted. The lord of this house, Jupiter, is located in 11th house in its own sign, Pisces. Further, Rahu and Moon from 2nd house aspect this house by their 7th aspect. 8th house represents longevity, falls, and obstacles, interests in archaeology and occult subjects. Planetary effects indicate that person would enjoy good health and have a long life. Exalted Ketu could confer some title, distinction or award on him during its (Ketu's) *dasha**.

In CK, sign of the 8th house is Capricorn and its Lord Saturn is located in its own sign in this house. Therefore, the overall planetary effects of JK and CK would be beneficial to the person for this house.

9th House

In JK, sign of this house is Capricorn. Saturn, the lord of this house and the lord of 10th house is located in this house. This is an important Raj Yoga, i.e. the lord of 9th house (*Mooi-Trikon*) and 10th House (Kendra) being in the 9th house in its own sign. 9th house represents good fortune, spiritual inclination, windfalls, journeys by air, relations with father etc. Saturn in its own sign in this house would make the person highly fortunate but he would lack any interest in spirituality. Whatever little interest he may have in spirituality would be masked since Saturn is a highly reserved and reticent planet. He would undertake many journeys by air. He would be helpful to father and would be helped by father in an unostentatious manner because of the reticent nature of Saturn.

In CK, the sign of 9th house is Aquarius and its lord Saturn is located in its own sign Capricorn (10) in 8th house. It is a general rule that any planet located in 8th house has a negative effect on the house of which it is a lord. However, Saturn, even though located in 8th house, is in its own sign Capricorn (10), therefore, its negative effect on the 9th house would be considerably diminished.

Overall, since the LK is much stronger than CK for the 9th house, the combined effects of LK and CK would be beneficial and positive for the person.

10th House

Sign of this house is Aquarius and its lord, Saturn, is located in its own sign (Capricorn) in 9th house. The house is fully aspected by a powerful Mars in sign Scorpio from 7th house by its 4th aspect or *drishti*. 10th house represents one's profession, business, public standing, reputation, relation with government, father etc. Saturn, the lord of this house is very powerful, being located in its own sign in the house of fortune (9th house) would have an extremely beneficial effect on this house. Again, Mars, being located in its own sign in 7th house (Kendra) is very powerful, would have a hugely beneficial effect on this house.

In CK, sign of 10th house is Pisces (12) and its lord Jupiter is located in this house in its own sign. This is a strong position for the beneficial Jupiter and would be extremely beneficial for the 10th house. However, Jupiter in this house is fully aspected by Saturn from 8th house by its 3rd aspect and that aspect of Saturn would tend to undermine Jupiter as Saturn is unfriendly to Jupiter. Thus, the overall beneficial effect of Jupiter on this house would be somewhat diminished.

Overall, the combined effect of JK and CK on 10th house would be excellent. Person would hold a high position in government service. When 3 planets especially Mars, Saturn and Jupiter either aspect 10th house or are located there, they tend to make such a person a medical man or a surgeon.

11th House

In JK, sign of 11th house is Pisces and its lord Jupiter is located in this house in its own sign. This is a very strong position for Jupiter. 11th house is the house of gains, regular income, prosperity and victory over enemies. A powerful Jupiter would confer all these benefits on the person.

In CK, the sign of 11th house is Aries and its lord Mars is located in its own sign (Scorpio) in 6th house in conjunction with Venus. Also, this house is fully aspected by Sun and Mercury from 5th house in CK by their 7th aspect. 11th house represents gains and regular income such as salary. Overall effects would be that person would have very high income from multiple sources, i.e. 2 to 3 sources. Person would also gain from his enemies – the effect of Mars in its own sign in 6th house (house of enemies) and also being the lord of 11th house (house of income) in CK.

Overall, the combined effects of LK and CK would be highly beneficial for the person in respect of the 11th house, i.e., income and gains.

12th House

In JK, the sign of 12th house is Aries and its lord Mars is situated in its own sign in 7th house (Kendra) in conjunction with Venus. Further, this house is fully aspected by Sun and Mercury from 6th house by their 7th aspect or drishti. Mars in its own sign Scorpio is quite powerful and Venus in neutral sign Scorpio is helpful. Sun in its sign of debilitation, Libra, in the 6th house is quite weak and unhelpful for the 12th house. Mercury in in its friendly sign, Libra, in 6th house is quite helpful for the 12th house. 12th house represents losses, worries, expenses, travels etc., the planetary effects of Mars and Venus and Mercury would be helpful for this house but the effect of Sun would be quite unhelpful.

In CK, sign of 12 the house is Taurus and its lord Venus is located in 6th house in conjunction with Mars in sign Scorpio. Mars in its own sign, Scorpio, is very powerful and Venus in its neutral sign, Scorpio is somewhat helpful for the 12th house and both of them fully aspect the 12th house by their 7th aspect. 12th house represents expenses, losses, one's worries and anxieties, foreign lands etc. Overall, effect of Mars and Venus would be positive for this house. Thus the person would have high expenses and suffer unexpected losses. Overall, the combined effects of JK and CK may lead to very high expenses, unexpected losses, multiple travels by sea and air to foreign lands, a strong attraction for foreign lands and may settle abroad for work.

Consideration of lagan *Kundli* and *Navansh Kundli* together

Navamsh Kundli (NK) is a very important chart which needs to be taken into consideration for the purpose of making a prediction. It gives a more detailed and a high-power microscopic view of the signs and placements of planets in the lagan *kundli* (LK). The initial prediction based on assessment of LK alone would very often get considerably modified when this assessment is combined with assessment of NK. NK acts very much in the manner of fine-tuning and modulating the notes generated by LK.

Illustrating the effects of *Navansh Kundli* on the findings of lagan *Kundli*
Example

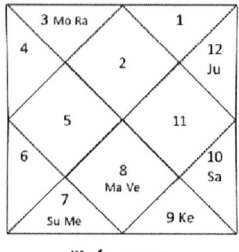

JK of a person

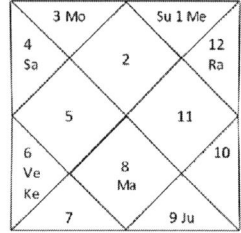

NK of a person

Janam Kundli (JK) and *Navamsh Kundli* (NK) of a person are placed side by side in the above two diagrams for the purpose of illustration. Points which need to be made a special note of include:

Ascendant

1. In LK, Taurus is the sign of the ascendant. In NK, Taurus again, happens to be the sign of the ascendant. This is known as a "*Vargottami Navamsh*". When the signs of ascendant in JK and NK are identical, it is known as *Vargottami Navamsh*. This confers a kind of "special status" on the person in that he outshines everyone else in the clan and is an outstanding personality.
2. In LK, the lord of the sign of ascendant is Venus and it is placed in the 7th house (Kendra) in its neutral sign Scorpio. Venus is in conjunction with Mars in the 7th house in sign Scorpio. Mars, being the lord of this house imparts a lot of strength to Venus. Venus derives further strength as it is placed in a Kendra (7th house). Venus also aspects the ascendant directly by its 7th aspect.

Based on the above 2 points in LK, one may conclude that the ascendant of the person is very strong.

3. In NK, Venus is debilitated in sign Virgo in the 5th house. Debilitated lord of ascendant in NK, significantly weakens the lord of ascendant. Debilitated Venus is in 5th house in NK; 5th house is generally considered good for placement of all planets. However, even its placement in 5th house cannot mitigate the weakness of Venus due to its debilitation.

   So, a consideration of LK and NK leads one to conclude that the ascendant of the person is weak. This weakness is mitigated to some extent by virtue of the fact that the *Navamsh* of the person is *Vargottmi*.

   Overall, the debilitation of lord of ascendant noted in NK would have the effect of reducing the will power and decision-making capacity of the person.

4. In JK, Sun is debilitated in sign Libra in 6h house. However, in NK, Sun is exalted in sign Aries in 12th house. This means that the ill-effects of Sun noted in JK, are mitigated to a very large extent by an exalted Sun in NK. Thus the bad effects of Sun concerning relations with mother noted in JK would be offset by the exalted Sun in NK; consequently, person would have very good relations with mother but may live away from her due to the position of Sun in 12th house in NK.

5. Another feature of note is that the planets Moon and Mars have identical signs in LK and
   NK. This makes these two planets very powerful or *Vargottmi*. They would show their best effects during the periods of their reign, i.e. their *mahadasha*, *antardasha* and *praytantradasha*.

6. Jupiter is in its own sign Pisces in LK and it is again in its own sign Sagittarius in NK. So, overall, Jupiter remains strong for the person. However, its

placement in 8th house in NK takes away some of its merits.

7. Saturn, lord of 9th house and 10th house, is in 9th house in JK and is "*Rajyog Karak*", being lord of *Mooi-Trikon* (9th house) and 10th house (Kendra). However, in NK, Saturn is in inimical sign Cancer and that would take away some of its strength noted in JK. But Saturn is in 3rd house in NK and this is considered to be a very favourable position for it. Overall, Saturn would retain most of its strength noted in JK.

8. Mercury, lord of 2nd and 5th house is in friendly sign Libra in 6th house and is quite weak on account of its placement in the 6th house. It is placed in neutral sign Aries in 12th house in NK and remains quite weak due to its placement in 12th house. Therefore, overall, Mercury remains weak in respect of its effects on 2nd house and 5th house of which it is the lord.

GOCHAR KUNDLI OR CHART

Gochar* kundli or chart depicts the current position of the planets at any point in time. On an average, *Nakshytra+* changes every day, Moon stays in one sign for two and a half days, Mars stays in a sign for a variable period, may be a month, less or more, Mercury again for a variable period of 1month, less or more, Jupiter for approximately 13 months, Venus for 1 month, less or more, Saturn for two and a half years and Sun for 1month in a sign.

It is important to remember that *Gochar Kundli* (GK) needs to be considered whenever presented with a horoscope chart for prediction.

This point is being brought out by the following example.